SYLVIA PLATH

Her Life and Work

Eileen M. Aird

PERENNIAL LIBRARY

Harper & Row, Publishers

New York, Evanston, San Francisco, London

This book was published in 1973 by Harper & Row, Publishers,
Inc., Barnes & Noble Import Division.
It is here reprinted by arrangement.

First PERENNIAL LIBRARY edition published 1975

STANDARD BOOK NUMBER: 06–080341–X

75 2

SYLVIA PLATH

the text of this book is printed on 100% recycled paper

For Edwin

Contents

Acknowledgments

The author and publishers are grateful to Ted Hughes and Olwyn Hughes and to Faber and Faber Ltd. for permission to quote from the works of Sylvia Plath.

1   Introduction

Tragically Sylvia Plath's work only gained recognition after her death. The one collection of poetry published in her lifetime, *The Colossus*, gained only fair reviews, as did *The Bell Jar*, and it is still on the work written in the last eighteen months of her life that her reputation chiefly relies. This was not collected until two years after her premature death. During the last few months of her life some of the late poems were published in journals and newspapers, particularly *London Magazine* and *The New Statesman*, and no doubt discriminating readers already appreciated the painful originality of her work. *The Observer*, whose poetry editor, A. Alvarez, was one of the earliest to recognise Sylvia Plath's talent, published a few poems during her lifetime and many after her death. However it was not until *Ariel* was published in 1965 that she was widely acclaimed. By this time *The Colossus* was out of print in the original Heinemann edition but it was reissued by Faber and Faber in 1967 as a result of the popularity of *Ariel*. *The Bell Jar*, published by Heinemann under the pseudonym of Victoria Lucas in 1963, was also unavailable when *Ariel* was published but Faber eventually reissued it under Sylvia Plath's own name. Her fame developed steadily from 1965 onwards and with the publication of two further collections in 1971, *Crossing the Water* and *Winter Trees*, it is now possible to trace very clearly the development of her work from late 1958 to early 1963.

This development is a quite extraordinary one by any standards; from the delicate, assured skills of *The Colossus*, through the tentative but striking experiments of *Crossing the Water* to the final achievement of *Winter Trees* and *Ariel*. However, despite the complete change of tone and style, the unity of Sylvia Plath's work is clear. The restrained concerns of *The Colossus* are illuminated by the fierce energy of *Ariel*; both are stages in one progression. Ted Hughes has underlined the necessity for studying the individual poems as one element in a complex but unified whole:[1]

> Surveyed as a whole, with attention to the order of composition, I think the unity of her opus is clear. Once the unity shows itself, the logic and inevitability of the language, which controls and contains such conflagrations and collisions within itself, becomes more obviously what it is – direct, even plain, speech.

Sylvia Plath's background and experience are of particular importance to our understanding of the work, much of which relies on some biographical knowledge. The developing strategy and technique of her work was based on the desire to analyse and lay bare the dilemmas and contrasts of her own, often painful, experience. She was an American married to an Englishman who is also a considerable poet in his own right and her work has important affinities with both American and European literature. She felt herself to be particularly involved with recent European experience and thought because of her own European descent and her work reveals this concern. This attitude is the antithesis of the conventional American response to European culture as an enigmatic, desirable but ultimately alien pattern.

The poet was born on 27 October 1932 in Boston, Massachusetts, of a mixed American–European parentage. Otto Emil Plath, Sylvia's father, emigrated to America from Grabow, a town in the Polish corridor, at the age of fifteen. Her mother, Aurelia Schober, was a first-generation American of Austrian descent. Both parents were academics; Otto Plath being a Professor at Boston University with a specialist interest in bees. This family background with its regard for academic prowess undoubtedly influenced Sylvia Plath's own intense desire for educational distinction. Ted Hughes has written of his wife's early life:[2]

> 'She grew up in an atmosphere of tense intellectual competition and Germanic rigour.'

1. 'Notes on the Chronological Order of Sylvia Plath's Poems', Ted Hughes in *The Art of Sylvia Plath*, p. 195.
2. *Poetry Book Society Bulletin*, 1966, p. 1.

The Plaths lived at the coast in the town of Winthrop, Massachusetts. Aurelia Plath's own parents, the Schobers, lived near by at Point Shirley, facing the bay on one side and the open sea on the other and within sight of Deer Island prison. In a talk written for the BBC, 'Ocean 1212-W'[3] Sylvia Plath described this area and dwelt on her nostalgic memories of a childhood world romantically defined by the sea. When her daughter was two Mrs Plath gave birth to a son, Warren Joseph, on 27 April 1935. The older child must have felt herself rejected and possibly replaced by this new arrival: this is the way she phrased the matter at any rate with the retrospective humour of adulthood:[4]

> 'A baby! I hated babies. I who for two and a half years had been the centre of a tender universe felt the axis wrench and a polar chill immobilize my bones. I would be a bystander, a museum mammoth. Babies!'

This feeling is perhaps sophisticatedly analysed from indistinct childhood memories by the adult aware of Freud and Spock, and she indicates in her talk that the younger brother quickly became her accepted companion in the childhood seaside life of learning to swim, helping an older cousin build a boat and eating the sea-food dishes lovingly prepared by the Viennese grandmother.

When Sylvia Plath was five a tidal hurricane hit the New England coast. The poet remembers it as occurring in 1939, but although there may have been a minor one that year the force of the one described in 'Ocean 1212-W' suggests that she is actually remembering the great hurricane of 21 September 1938, which was described in a report in *The Times*:

'A tropical hurricane which struck with full force yesterday at Long Island and then raged through New England into Canada resulted in the loss of over 200 lives and damage to property estimated at £100,000,000 . . .'

The young child exulted in the excitement of the hurricane which

3. *The Listener*, 29 August 1963, pp. 312–3.
4. *Ibid.* p. 312.

buffeted and threatened the house during the night, and relished the next day's signs of destruction:[5]

> The wreckage the next day was all one could wish –
> overthrown trees and telephone poles, shoddy summer
> cottages bobbing out by the lighthouse, and a litter of
> the ribs of little ships. My grandmother's house had
> lasted valiant – though the waves broke right over the
> road and into the bay. My grandfather's sea-wall had
> saved it, neighbours said. Sand buried her furnace in
> golden whorls; salt stained the upholstered sofa, and a
> dead shark filled what had been the geranium bed, but
> my grandmother had her broom out, it would soon be
> right.

Here the poet in reconstructing the child's vision sees the grandmother as more than a match for the ravages of the mere elements, but in describing the same episode in 'Point Shirley' she sees the surge and vitality of her grandmother's life as finally and darkly conquered by the natural elements concentrated in death. Memories of the idyllic childhood are constantly distorted by the rigours of the adult's vision.

Sylvia Plath's father died after a long and difficult illness when she was nine. Ted Hughes has written that she 'worshipped her father',[6] and his death was clearly an event of major importance in her life, which was to assume significance as an obscure, disturbing, yet dominant element in her poetry. After the death of her husband Aurelia Plath combined her family with that of her parents and they all moved inland to Wellesley, a pretty, tree-lined, upper middle-class suburb of Boston. The seaside childhood was over although it was later to be recalled as a time of remote, perfect happiness:[7]

> And this is how it stiffens, my vision of that seaside
> childhood. My father died, we moved inland. Whereon
> those nine first years of my life sealed themselves off

5. *Ibid.* p. 313.
6. *Poetry Book Society Bulletin*, 1966, p. 1.
7. 'Ocean 1212-W', p. 313.

like a ship in a bottle – beautiful, inaccessible,
obsolete, a fine, white, flying myth.

Sylvia Plath dated her interest in poetry from her early childhood when she remembered her mother reading aloud Mathew
Arnold's 'Forsaken Merman'; she responded immediately and
intensely. Her own first publication appeared in a Boston news-
paper when she was eight and a half:

> Hear the crickets chirping
> In the dewy grass.
> Bright little fireflies
> Twinkle as they pass.

Hardly an indication of her adult talent it nevertheless shows a
pleasing awareness of rhythm and rhyme. It is the poem of a
child aware of and responsive to her natural surroundings, and
she later described the subject of this and other early childhood
poems as:[8]

> Nature, I think: birds, bees, spring, fall, all those
> subjects which are absolute gifts to the person who
> doesn't have any interior experience to write about.
> I think the coming of spring, the stars overhead, the
> first snowfall and so on are gifts for a child, a young
> poet.

The attempt to define her perceptions of the external world is one
of the features of Sylvia Plath's first book *The Colossus*, and in the
light of her theory of nature as a subject for those without interior
experiences, it is significant to note that the work of her poetic
maturity moved away from the nature poems of *The Colossus*. Or
rather the indications of menace and stress which are contained in
the natural world of *The Colossus* are released in the *Ariel* universe,
where they dominate the poet's vision of both externals and
internals, so that when the natural world appears in the poems, as
it does say in the late bee sequence, it serves as a reflection of the
poet's emotions. Ultimately Sylvia Plath was able to fuse her

8. Peter Orr (ed.), *The Poet Speaks*, p. 167.

recreation of the external world with her intense, inner perceptions, creating a mythological, visionary world which was both grotesque and beautiful.

The poet was educated at the Marshall Livingston Grammar School and then at the Gamaliel Bradford Senior High. Her results and reports were consistently good and as she grew up the desire to write became a more compelling one which was accompanied by the need to see her name in print. The picture which emerges from the scanty information available on the adolescent Sylvia Plath is that of a normal, rather extrovert teenager developing her artistic and literary talents but not at the expense of social relationships and enjoyment. She was also developing intellectually; Ted Hughes has said of her academic career;[9]

> Whatever teaching methods were used Sylvia was the perfect pupil: she did every lesson double. Her whole tremendous will was bent on excelling. Finally, she emerged like the survivor of an evolutionary ordeal: at no point could she let herself be negligent or inadequate.

In September 1950 Sylvia Plath entered Smith College, which is both expensive and exclusive, on full scholarships. She worked hard to achieve high grades and took courses in French, Botany, Art, Government, History, Russian literature and English literature in which she majored. She also continued to write stories and poems and in 1952 won the *Mademoiselle* fiction contest with her short story 'Sunday at the Mintons'. When the news of her 500 dollar prize arrived she was scrubbing furniture in a Cape Cod hotel. Other vacation jobs she took while still a student included work as a picker on a vegetable farm, a job as a mother's help on Cape Cod and waitressing in a Smith cooperative house. She wrote that many of the characters she met during these jobs 'manage to turn up, dismembered or otherwise, in stories'.[10]

Six months later she followed the *Mademoiselle* prize with second prize in *Seventeen's* Fiction Contest. During the same year her poetry won two Smith poetry awards and her literary aspirations

9. *Poetry Book Society Bulletin*, 1966, p. 1.
10. *Mademoiselle*, August 1953, p. 291.

were greatly encouraged when she won a Guest Editorshop on *Mademoiselle*. This involved a paid trip to New York and a salaried job in *Mademoiselle*'s Madison Avenue offices during June. The guest editors went to parties and theatres and interviewed celebrities in their fields of interest. Sylvia Plath was Guest Managing Editor. One of her assignments on the magazine was to write a correspondence article on five young poets—Anthony Hecht, Alastair Reid, Richard Wilbur, George Steiner and William Burford—which was printed under the title of 'Poets on the Campus'. The magazine also contains a picture of Sylvia Plath interviewing the novelist Elizabeth Bowen; the picture shows her as pretty, apparently self-composed and vivacious. This magazine is further important as being the source of one of her earliest poems, 'A Mad Girl's Love-Song', and her literary versatility is illustrated by the fashion and gossip column which she wrote under the heading '*Mademoiselle*'s Last Word on College 1953'. Its easy flippancy is a far cry from the tortured poetry of *Ariel* but the maintained astronomical imagery perhaps indicates a more developed literary talent than is usually found in fashion columnists.

After the weeks in New York Sylvia Plath returned to Wellesley for the rest of the summer vacation. During these weeks she became intensely depressed and eventually attempted suicide by swallowing a large number of sleeping pills before hiding herself in the cellar beneath the house. Luckily she was still alive, although very ill, when she was found three days later. Her discovery was followed by hospital treatment, including electro-convulsive therapy, but by mid-winter her doctors considered her well enough to return to Smith. Despite these events she fulfilled her academic promise by graduating *summa cum laude* in 1955 and winning a Fulbright scholarship to Cambridge, England. At Cambridge she was an external student affiliated to Newnham College from 1955–7. In 1957 she took the second part of the English tripos, graduating with an upper second class honours degree. When she graduated from Cambridge she was already married to the poet Ted Hughes. They met in Cambridge in February, 1956 and were married in London on 16 June of the same year. Sylvia Plath modestly gave her 'rank or profession' as 'student', but her husband more firmly gave 'writer'. Ted Hughes' background was quite different from that of Sylvia Plath.[11] Born on 17 August 1930 in the small town of Mytholmroyd in the West Riding of Yorkshire, he was the youngest of three children, having both a brother and a sister. His father, William Henry Hughes, was a carpenter at the time of his younger son's birth, but when Ted Hughes was seven the family moved to Mexborough, a more industrial town in south Yorkshire, where the Hughes took a tobacconist's and newsagent's shop. Ted Hughes was educated at Mexborough Grammar School, and in 1948 won an Open Exhibition in English to Pembroke College, Cambridge. Before going up to Cambridge he did two years' national service on an isolated three man radio station in east Yorkshire.

In 1953 Hughes took part one of the English tripos, but in his final year he read the Archeology and Anthropology tripos. His experience of Cambridge does not seem to have been an altogether happy one and he has written of the opposition which he sees between a formal, academic education and the desire to write. After graduating Hughes wandered around for two years doing casual jobs in various places:[12]

> I graduated in 1954. After a spell of teaching here and there, and another driving an uncle around the continent, I took a job as a rose-gardener, then as a night watchman in a steel factory in London, and later as a reader for J. Arthur Rank at the Pinewood Studios.

In 1956, after his marriage to Sylvia Plath, Ted Hughes took a job in a secondary modern school in Cambridge while his wife completed her studies. They spent the summer after their marriage in Benidorm, a small fishing village on the Mediterranean, now a considerable resort but then unspoilt; some of the earlier poems in *The Colossus* date from this period, and Hughes has described 'Departure' as being 'a memory of Benidorm'.[13] They returned to Cambridge for the beginning of the academic year and lived in a

11. Most of the biographical information about Ted Hughes appears in an autobiographical note on the files of *The Halifax Courier and Guardian*.

12. *Ibid.*

13. Hughes, 'Notes on the Chronological Order of Sylvia Plath's Poems', *op. cit.*, p. 188.

small flat overlooking Grantchester Meadows. Before this time Hughes had published little but his wife began to submit his poems to magazines and journals and during 1957 he had several poems published and made a recording of Yeats' poems and one of his own for the BBC Third Programme. Sylvia Plath had already published poems in America as an undergraduate and during this year she had several accepted for publication, particularly by *Poetry*.

In 1957 the Hughes left for America to spend the summer on Cape Cod, before going on to Northampton, Massachusetts, where Sylvia Plath had a job as an instructor in English at Smith College, where she was to teach in their introductory course in English composition and critical writing. While his wife taught freshman English at Smith, Ted Hughes taught creative writing and literary courses at the University of Massachusetts. Sylvia Plath said of their teaching experiences:[14]

> Ted and I had similar reactions. It was exciting and rewarding to introduce students to writers one particularly enjoys, to stimulate discussions and to watch students develop, but it takes time and energy. Too much, we found, to be able to work at any length on any writing of our own.

Consequently they decided to relinquish their university jobs and to spend 1958–9 writing and living on Beacon Hill in a small apartment. Their experiences were very similar during this period of literary exploration and development even though their poetry was developing in quite different directions:[15]

> Both of us want to write as much as possible, and we do. Ted likes a table he made in a window niche from two planks, and I have a fetish about my grandmother's desk with an ivy and grape design burned into the wood. In the morning we have coffee (a concession to America) and in the afternoon tea (a concession to England.) That's about the extent of our

14. 'Four Young Poets', *Mademoiselle*, January 1959, p. 35.
15. *Ibid.*

differences. We do criticise each other's work, but we write poems that are as distinct and different as our fingerprints themselves must be.

During this year in Boston Sylvia Plath began to attend Robert Lowell's poetry classes at Boston University. Here she met the American poets George Starbuck and Anne Sexton. Anne Sexton remembers that one recurrent subject of conversation was suicide. She shared with Sylvia Plath the experience of attempted suicide and nervous breakdown, and they seem to have indulged with morbid fervour in lengthy recreations of their similar experiences:[16]

> Sylvia and I often talked opposites. We talked death with burned-up intensity, both of us drawn to it like moths to an electric light bulb. Sucking on it! She told the story of her first suicide in sweet and loving detail and her description in *The Bell Jar* is just the same story.

In this year when neither of them worked regularly the Hughes lived on their savings, implemented by income from occasional poetry readings, publications and small jobs. Among other temporary appointments Sylvia Plath worked for a time as a secretary to a Boston psychiatrist; this experience is clearly reflected in two of her short stories: 'The Daughters of Blossom Street' and 'Johnny Panic and the Bible of Dreams'. Then in the spring of 1959 Hughes was awarded a Guggenheim Fellowship and they spent that summer hiking across America, camping out at nights. In September they were invited to spend some time at Saratoga Springs, New York, donated by Mrs Katrina Peabody as a refuge for creative artists. Guests usually arrive during the summer and remain there for a month or two free of charge. Ted Hughes recalls that there were only two or three residents there during their stay, and these weeks produced the last of the poems in *The Colossus*, including 'Poem For a Birthday'. They were now expecting their first child and in December, 1959 the

16. 'The Barfly Ought to Sing', *Tri-Quarterly*, Fall 1966, p. 104. Included in *The Art of Sylvia Plath*, p. 175.

Hughes returned to England, intending to settle permanently in Europe.

In February 1960 they moved into a flat in a small square near Primrose Hill. Frieda Rebecca, their first child, was born here on 1 April 1960. Shortly after returning to England Sylvia Plath had submitted the manuscript of *The Colossus* to Heinemann on 25 January 1960 and on 10 February the contract was made out. In March of that year Ted Hughes won the Somerset Maugham award and shortly afterwards his second book of poems, *Lupercal*, was awarded the Hawthornden prize. Clearly their literary ambitions were coming to fruition and were providing them with income. It was at about this time that Sylvia Plath began to write *The Bell Jar*, partly supported by the Martha Saxton award which she had recently won. *The Colossus* was duly published on 31 October 1960 but the following winter was a bad one for Sylvia Plath who had a miscarriage, followed by an appendectomy and then became pregnant in spring 1961. Nevertheless during this time she completed her novel which was submitted to Heinemann at the end of August 1961. In August she also heard that she had won first prize in the Cheltenham Festival Poetry Competition with her poem 'Insomniac'. At the invitation of the organiser, Eric White of the Arts Council, she donated the manuscript of *Insomniac* to the British Museum, writing from Chalcot Square: 'I am happy to enclose the work sheets of *Insomniac*, and happy to hear from the Cheltenham Festival Organisers that sleeplessness has its own very pleasant reward.' The manuscript of the poem is much revised, consisting of several sheets of handwritten versions and a final typescript which is also altered. The first draft is written on the back of a sheet of British Museum typing paper, on which part of 'Poem for a Birthday' was typed and then crossed out, suggesting that Sylvia Plath, like so many other writers, worked in the Museum Reading Room.

In the summer of 1961 the Hughes left London to live in an old manor house in an isolated village in Devon. Although writing was now taking up a great deal of her time Sylvia Plath was also a wife and mother; she did housework and gardening with enthusiasm and cared for her daughter efficiently and well as she did everything. In January 1962 her son, Nicholas Farrar Hughes, was born. From this time dates a period of great creative fertility which Ted Hughes has specifically related to her experience of maternity:[17]

> With the birth of her first child she received herself,
> and was able to turn to her advantage all the forces of
> a highly-disciplined, highly intellectual style of
> education which had, up to this point, worked mainly
> against her, but without which she could hardly have
> gone so coolly into the regions she now entered. The
> birth of her second child, in January of 1962, completed
> the preparation.

Whatever the reason this last year of her life witnessed a creative abundance of work, including most of the *Winter Trees* and *Ariel* poems. She also continued to look after house and children and under the tuition of her friend the local midwife learnt how to keep bees and make honey.

At the end of October 1962 Sylvia Plath went up to London at the invitation of the British Council to make a recording of her poetry. She read from a sheaf of manuscripts of her most recent poems. The poet was interviewed by Peter Orr of the British Council who remembers being impressed by her charm, intellect and vivacity of personality. A month later she wrote to him from Devon:[18]

> Thank you so much for the cheque and Stevie Smith's
> address—I've had delectably Smithish letter from the
> latter and hope I can meet her when I come up to
> London for good in a couple of weeks. I'm coming up
> again this Monday for a couple of days to make
> arrangements about my new place. It should amuse
> you with your shared mania for Ireland, that I'll be
> living in Yeats' house, plaque and all. The story is
> quite incredible and a bit witchy. I've always wanted
> to live in this particular house because of the Yeats'
> mania and on the one day I was up in London

17. Hughes, 'Notes on the Chronological Order of Sylvia Plath's Poems', *op. cit.*, p. 193.
18. The letter is in the possession of Mr Peter Orr.

happened to walk past, happened to see a signboard
out and the builders in and happened to be the first to
apply. When I got home, very cocky, I said to my
nurse 'I'll just open Yeats' *Plays* and get a message
about the house'. When I opened my eyes I was
pointing to the words 'Get food and wine and whatever
you need to give you strength and courage—and I will
get the house ready' from 'The Unicorn from the Stars'.
Well, if Willie wants to get in touch it is fine by me.
I think I'm a heck of a better sort than Dorothy
Wellesley. I'll send you the new address when I move
in so you can deluge me with Chesterton there, and a
book list of Victoriana, please. I may not be Eminent,
but my God, Victorian.

Unfortunately the meeting with Stevie Smith alluded to never
took place, although Miss Smith remembered receiving a letter
from Sylvia Plath. Sylvia Plath was coming up to London with her
children to live separately from Ted Hughes, although there was
some talk of her returning to the Devon house in the spring.
Unfortunately her tragic death intervened on 11 February 1963.
She was found with her head in the gas oven and was taken to
University College Hospital but was certified dead on arrival
there. The coroner's inquest was held four days later on the
fifteenth and the verdict returned was 'while suffering from
depression she did kill herself'.

She took her own life at what seemed to be the height of her
creative powers. *The Bell Jar* had been published on 14 January
and had been fairly well received, and she was writing up to two
or three poems a day. Her short life can be seen as a patterned and
recurrent conflict between external brilliance and achievement
and a deeper inner loneliness and conflict. She was practical and
efficient, everything the poet is traditionally not, but eventually
the inner chaos and loneliness were to overcome and subdue the
outer pattern. Her academic success, her marriage and children,
even her writing were not finally proof against the death which
alternately fascinated and frightened her and finally claimed her
at a tragically young age. Although her reputation has gradually
increased since her sad death, it is still inappropriate to attempt

any assessment of the 'greatness' of her work. Time alone can determine this. Her originality, however, lies in her insistence that what has been traditionally regarded as a woman's world of domesticity, childbearing, marriage, is also a world which can contain the tragic. She draws from this female world themes which are visionary and supernatural; although it is a world which is eventually destroyed by death, her work is far from depressing because of the artistry with which she delineates her vision. Yeats' statement: 'Out of the quarrel with ourselves we make poetry' seems a fitting epitaph for Sylvia Plath who died in his house.

2   *The Colossus*

The poems in *The Colossus*, the only collection of Sylvia Plath's poetry published during her lifetime, were all written between 1956 when she was reading English at Cambridge and the end of 1959 when she was about to return to England to live here permanently. Ted Hughes' article on the chronology of these poems[1] enables us to divide them into four groups. The first dates from the two years at Cambridge and includes 'Sow', 'Hardcastle Crags', 'Faun', 'Departure', 'All the Dead Dears', 'Watercolour of Grantchester Meadows', 'Strumpet Song', and 'Spinster'; the publication dates of 'Black Rook in Rainy Weather' and 'Two Sisters of Persephone' assign them to this group also. The second group belongs to the year 1957–8 when Sylvia Plath was teaching at Smith College. 'Mussel-Hunter at Rock Harbour' was written during the summer the Hughes spent on Cape Cod before the start of the academic year; 'Night Shift', 'Lorelei', 'The Thin People', 'The Ghost's Leavetaking', 'Full Fathom Five', 'Snake-charmer', 'The Disquieting Muses', 'Frog Autumn' and 'Sculptor' were written between autumn 1957, when she began to teach, and summer 1958, when she left Smith College. The following year of 1958 to summer 1959 was spent in Boston and dates the third group which comprises 'Two Views of a Cadaver Room', 'The Eye-Mote', 'Point Shirley', 'Aftermath', 'Suicide off Egg Rock', 'Man in Black', 'The Hermit at Outermost House', and 'The Beekeeper's Daughter'. The final and smallest group was written during the weeks Ted Hughes and Sylvia Plath spent at Yaddo in the late autumn of 1959. The poems of this time are 'The Manor Garden', 'Mushrooms', 'A Winter Ship', 'Blue Moles', 'The Burnt-Out Spa' and 'Poem for a Birthday'.

This chronological grouping leaves ten of the forty-four poems in *The Colossus* unaccounted for, although the publication dates of

1. Hughes, *op. cit.*, pp. 187–95.

'I Want, I Want', 'The Companionable Ills' and 'The Times are Tidy' indicate that these three poems do not belong to the fourth group but probably to the second or third. Of the remaining seven the most important are the title-poem and 'Moonrise'. The publication dates, style and subject of both poems suggest that they belong to one of the last two groups. I would tentatively assign 'The Colossus' to the third group. In his note on 'The Beekeeper's Daughter', with which 'The Colossus' was first published, Ted Hughes has said:[2] '"The Beekeeper's Daughter" is one of a group of poems that she wrote at this time about her father.' 'The Colossus' may well be one of the same group, as may the uncollected poem 'Electra on Azalea Path'.[3]

Although the poems in *The Colossus* end with 'Poem For a Birthday' which Hughes notes is the last poem his wife wrote at Yaddo, the book is not arranged chronologically. The first poem, 'The Manor Garden', belongs to the last group also. However the subject of the four groups does indicate a unity within each division which justifies discussion of them in this way; this strategy presents a clear picture of the considerable development in both style and treatment of subject from 'Sow', one of the earliest poems, to 'Poem For a Birthday'.

'Sow' is a light-hearted extravaganza on the magnificence of a prize pig which Sylvia Plath saw on a farm in Yorkshire. The admiration of the pig's spectators leads them to conjure up visions of the sow at the centre of some legendary triumph, but the farmer's proprietary nonchalance reveals pride of a more mundane order. The poem is chiefly distinctive by virtue of its vocabulary and form which are extreme examples of the stylistic 'cleverness' of Sylvia Plath's early poetry. The vocabulary reveals an instinct for the unusual which is never precious. In six lines Sylvia Plath successfully combines an archaism, a colloquialism and a literary allusion. 'Sow', in fact is a clever, witty development of circular fantasies on a very concrete theme in which the poet has revealed her ability to form a complex pattern of rhyme, metre and sound. The affirmative vigour of this poem is allowed to stand unqualified by the glancing withdrawal that would be charac-

2. *Ibid.*, p. 190.
3. 'Electra on Azalea Path', *Hudson Review*, 13, autumn 1960, p. 414.

teristic of the later work. Comparison with Ted Hughes' 'View of a Pig' seems inevitable and the complexity of Hughes' response emphasises the frivolity of 'Sow'.

In 'Sow' Sylvia Plath gives a virtuoso performance as a deft craftsman, a maker; in 'Black Rook in Rainy Weather' she meditates on the nature of her poetic insights. The moment of perception from which poetry springs is concentrated in the sudden recognition of beauty even in the commonplace; in this traditional moment of inspiration, the intuition of the poet leads him to imaginative unity with his object, although Sylvia Plath describes the experience not in terms of a state of heightened sensibility, but as an external assault on the senses by the sudden incandescence of the object. These insights give value to the barren stretches of time when inspiration is absent; the ability to perceive and create establishes or confirms individuality in an existence which threatens it; the poet sees the poetic moment as, 'a brief respite from fear of total neutrality'. This definition is continually restated in the poetry.

The subject of 'Black Rook in Rainy Weather' is more fundamental than that of 'Sow', but as in the lighter poem Sylvia Plath creates an intricate formal pattern which she handles with a sureness which saves it from artificiality. It seems that she had to work through this period of intense concentration on form to achieve the freedom of her later poetry. These poems of her early volume indicate a consciousness of herself as a poet, a craftsman, which is absorbed and transcended in the later work. An uncollected poem of the same period, 'On the Difficulty of Conjuring up a Dryad',[4] also considers the nature of the poetic process, now seen as an attempt to transform actuality by imposing on it the greater order of artistic insight. The dryad or muse of the title is the agent of poetic order but she cannot be simply summoned at will, the moment of inspiration is relied on by the poet because the 'cold vision' of the intellect will readily perceive any artificiality or sentimentality in her struggle to progress from the perception of concrete reality to a deeper awareness. The melancholic reflectiveness of 'Black Rook in Rainy Weather' has been replaced in this poem by a wryly humorous statement of the difficulties of the would-be poet and Sylvia Plath manipulates the shape of the

4. 'On the Difficulty of Conjuring Up A Dryad', *Poetry*, 90, 1957, p. 235.

poem with skill to include the conversational ease of the third
verse:

> My trouble, doctor, is: I see a tree,
> And that damn scrupulous tree won't practise wiles
>   To beguile sight:
>   E.g. by cant of light
>   Concoct a Daphne;
>   My tree stays tree.

The movement towards the definition of the nature of the
creative arts is accompanied by an attempt to understand the
position of the individual in the universe, most characteristically
seen in those poems which indicate the poet's reactions to the
natural world of vegetation and animal life. In 'Watercolour of
Grantchester Meadows' Sylvia Plath comments on the delicate,
detailed landscape with qualified approval. She finds the calm
beauty of such a landscape basically unsatisfying because it is
based on the sheltered peace of 'a country on a nursery plate',
although this superficial quality must also be distrusted as it
disguises a deeper malignancy beneath the flowery prettiness:

> Hedging meadows of benign
> Arcadian green
> The blood-berried hawthorn hides its spines with white.

Neither academic learning nor human love offer any protection to
the students who are seen as the native inhabitants of the area;
they cannot detect the predatory savagery which lurks beneath
the calm, and thus despite all their knowledge, symbolised by
their black gowns, they are seriously limited by their unawareness
that the world contains not only their 'moony indolence of love',
but also a dark savagery in which 'The owl shall stoop from his
turret, the rat cry out'. The allegiances of the poet are ambivalent; the latent menace of the landscape subtly mocks its superficial prettiness and the delicate scale of the classical pastoral
scene dwindles into insignificance beside the bleaker grandeur of
the crueller world.

In 'Hardcastle Crags' Sylvia Plath describes her reactions to her
husband's native Yorkshire and reveals the same recognition of

unease. Hardcastle Crags is a large, wooded, rocky valley opening up from a small industrial town and finally merging into the Pennine moors. The poet walks out at night from a hilltop village into the open countryside, but frightened by the oppressive silence and contained menace of the night, she quickly returns to the village, feeling that her very being is threatened by the dormant stoniness of the dark night. The village represents the security of a human community which should provide some refuge against the blind, crushing indifference of nature but it is itself presented with some ambivalence. References to the 'steely street', 'The stone-built town' and 'the dark dwarfed cottages' suggest that the village itself is contaminated by the threat of the stony land beyond. However the 'firework of echoes' which her footsteps arouse in the quiet village seems preferable to the eeriness broken only by the babble of the wind which comes down around her in the fields, where there is movement, a strange, self-engrossed, wavelike dance of the grasses, but little sound. Her apprehension takes no familiar form, resolves itself into no recurrent nightmare but she is acutely aware of the pressure of natural forces which reduce her being to complete insignificance; her consciousness becomes an unwilling medium for the sleeping yet dominant nature around her:

> All the night gave her, in return
> For the paltry gift of her bulk and the beat
> Of her heart was the humped indifferent iron
> Of its hills, and its pastures bordered by black stone set
> On black stone.

Man seems to have made no impression on this stony landscape—the barns, animals, cultivated fields, which are evidence of man's existence are frozen into still sleep—and she flees from the hills which will subdue her into one more component of the stony scene.

Langbaum's theory of the poetry of experience illuminates the type of poetry which Sylvia Plath was already writing at this stage. Her later work is inescapably poetry of this order which seeks to recognise and know the essence of the other by imaginative identification with it. However the technique appears more simply in her earlier work in a poem such as 'Departure' where the persona sees her emotional reactions to a specific situation reflected in her surroundings, and finds the hostility of the financial circumstance, which is operative in the subjective world, matched by nature's rejection of her in the external world. In 'All the Dead Dears' the poet would like to reject the knowledge of experience in favour of the greater comfort of rational analysis which demonstrates the difference between living and dead; but as this difference is merely temporary she must accept the awareness of mortality revealed in her identification with the skeleton of a fourth-century woman seen in a museum. A raw awareness of the mortality of the frail individual in the face of the implacable, enduring, at times vengeful natural world is a constant theme of Sylvia Plath's poetry. The necessity of formulating a meaningful way of living a transient life forms the subject of two similar poems of this first group, 'Two Sisters of Persephone' and 'Spinster'. There are two possible reactions; one of withdrawal into a frosty and disciplined self-enclosure, where intellectual effort seeks to impose order; the other of a wholehearted sensuous and emotional participation. The first is chosen by the spinster who thus places herself beyond the reach of violence but also of love. The two sisters of the other poem adopt opposing attitudes, and the spiritual and physical fertility of the one is compared with the barren bitterness of the other, for whom the intellectual absolute is finally unavailing.

The poetry of experience seeks to appropriate and assimilate external reality by imaginative identification with it, but the act of self-projection cannot always end in sympathetic knowledge of, or unity with the object; it may reveal to the individual the extent of his alienation from the other and his enclosure in an insuperable difference. 'Mussel Hunter at Rock Harbour', one of the finest poems in the volume and the first in the second group, describes an attempt to penetrate and understand the motives and nature of another form of life which ends in a recognition of the impossibility of ever achieving such an awareness. The poet goes in the early morning to gather fish-bait on a deserted beach—Sylvia Plath was a keen fisherman—the lack of human activity deepens her perceptions of the strange otherworld of fish and animal life around her, and she rejects the painter's visual recreation of certain aspects of the scene for a close concentration on the elemental, living organisms to whom the beach belongs at this early hour. An undisturbed concentration sharpens the awareness of all her senses, but this awareness is undermined by a feeling that some inner mystery of the otherworld has rejected her:

> The mussels hung dull blue and
> Conspicuous, yet it seemed
> A sly world's hinges had swung
> Shut against me. All held still.

As she waits silently and without moving the crabs begin to emerge again and confirm her sense that she is separated from true knowledge of them. Her ability to describe their external movement and behaviour is not accompanied by any penetration of senses and awareness:

> . . . . They moved
> Obliquely with a dry-wet
> Sound, with a glittery wisp
> And trickle. Could they feel mud
> Pleasurable under claws

> As I could between bare toes?
> That question ended it—I
> Stood shut out, for once, for all,
> Puzzling the passage of their
> Absolutely alien
> Order . . .

This first poem of the second group is already stylistically quite different from the earlier 'Sow'. Ted Hughes has pointed out[5] that in 'Mussel Hunter at Rock Harbour' Sylvia Plath first used syllabics, and this simplicity of metre is accompanied by an overall ease and freedom of composition. The intricate, clever rhymes of 'Sow' have gone, although the poem is still divided into regular verse units; in the division of the poem into regular verses is the one stylistic device which Sylvia Plath maintained throughout her poetry;

5. Hughes, *op. cit.*, p. 189.

poems such as 'Getting There' and 'Lesbos' which abandon this regular division are the exception not the rule. The vocabulary of the Cambridge years which was original, vigorous and often witty in the metaphysical sense, has been modified into a less flamboyant approximation to spoken English without losing any of its earlier force.

'The Ghost's Leavetaking' suggests a quite different otherworld. The poem describes the two levels of imaginative activity found in the dream world and the conscious daily world and the impossibility of ever fusing the two for longer than the moment when the concrete world of objects and activity begins to supplant that world: 'Of sulphurous landscapes and obscure lunar conundrums/ Which seemed, when dreamed, to mean so profoundly much.' It is suggested that the otherworld of dreams is the more intense one, which furnishes some basis for conscious activity, but ultimately the poem is a less effective, because less serious treatment of its subject than 'Mussel Hunter at Rock Harbour'. It ends not with an attempt to explore the significance and nature of the dream world and its exact relation to the conscious world, but with an escape into a nursery rhyme reference which reduces the last line into a perhaps deliberately grandiose evasion.

A much denser poem is 'Sculptor', dedicated to Leonard Baskin whose work occasioned it. As well as revealing Sylvia Plath's fascination with the figures of Baskin's sculpture, it explores more deeply her conception of art and the role the artist plays in relation to his fellow human beings. He is seen in this poem as a medium, who, through his creation, gives life to a world which then eclipses the human world in which he exists. The paradox is that without the artist the created art could not exist, but once given form it attains a permanence, an absolute being, which outlasts the artist. Sylvia Plath makes a plea for the artist as interpreter, as a man who can communicate his insights to a world which can appreciate without being able to share his originality. The 'bald angel' of Baskin's work, which Sylvia Plath describes in 'Sculptor', finds a counterpart in a poem of the same period, 'The Disquieting Muses', which also embodies her developing conception of the nature and origin of art, but is further noteworthy as being one of the first of her autobiographical poems. The reference to the hurricane in the third verse recalls the 1938 hurricane which hit the New England coast in the poet's childhood and the other details of early experience are probably equally authentic. 'The Disquieting Muses' of the title are an evocation of the forces which the poet saw behind her work. The description of them as 'Mouthless, eyeless with stitched bald head' recalls not only the 'bald angel' of 'Sculptor' but also the mutilations of Hiroshima and Dachau which figure so prominently in the later poetry. The poet states that the bleak muses have been inhabitants of her world since birth and their influence in childhood cast a dark shadow over the world of normality and domesticity, in which her mother's witches 'always/Got baked into gingerbread', thus rendering them harmless. Allegiance to the muses became stronger as the child grew up and gave rise to the lack of social ease which so distressed the mother. Eventually the two worlds of comfortable normality and darker insight became irreconcilable in their demands, and the persona, finding the mother's world inconsequential and frivolous, made a deliberate choice of the world governed by the muses, even though it opposes stony blankness to the bright gaiety of the mother's world of balloons, flowers and bluebirds:

> Day now, night now, at head, side, feet,
> They stand their vigil in gowns of stone,
> Faces blank as the day I was born,
> Their shadows long in the setting sun
> That never brightens or goes down.
> And this is the kingdom you bore me to,
> Mother, mother. But no frown of mine
> Will betray the company I keep.

'Lorelei' and 'Full Fathom Five', companion poems written during this year, introduce a new and disturbing element into the poetry. Hughes notes[6] that both poems were prompted by a reading of one of Cousteau's accounts of his diving and underwater exploration, but the source is incidental; the poems are much more than descriptive, they become vehicles for the expression of the complex, fearful fascination with death which is a recurrent motif in Sylvia Plath's work from this point onwards.

6. *Ibid.*, p. 189.

Both poems employ the three line verse which is one of her most characteristic modes, both in *The Colossus* and the later poems. 'Lorelei' describes a river at night, 'Full Fathom Five'—the reference to Ariel's song which tells Ferdinand of his father's supposed death is significant—the sea at dawn. In 'Lorelei' the sleeping peace of the human world is broken by the song of the Rhine-maidens who offer 'a world more full and clear/Than can be'. The poet sees this underwater world as containing a promise of a life 'Beyond the mundane order', which will transform the boredom and monotony of daily life into an eternal peace. Even though she associates the Rhine maidens with 'the pitched reefs of nightmare' her final longing is for unity with this world, although this must involve personal death. The complexity of a response which includes both fear and desire is stated more clearly in 'Full Fathom Five'. The old man who rises from the sea is disfigured by some terrible yet vague injury and although he is associated with the eternal presence of the sea, his being is also rooted in the tangible reminders of dead mortals. Nevertheless the persona longs, as in 'Lorelei', for unity with this spirit through death:

> You defy other godhood.
> I walk dry on your kingdom's border
> Exiled to no good.
>
> Your shelled bed I remember.
> Father, this thick air is murderous.
> I would breathe water.

The poems of these first two groups reveal the desire to define the relationship between self and the outside world, and also indicate the poet's wish to come to terms with the concept of art and the relationship between the abstract absolute and the individual's vision of it. The poems of the third group, written in the year following her decision to relinquish an academic career for writing and marriage, begin to treat personal and painful experience as poetic subjects. The material of many of these poems also appears in *The Bell Jar*, and they can be seen as resulting from the confrontation between the poet's memories of her childhood and adolescence in the area in which she was now living as a married adult, and the perceptions which her absence had generated. The experience described in 'Two Views of a Cadaver Room' corresponds to Esther Greenwood's visit to Buddy Willard's laboratory, while 'Suicide Off Egg Rock' bears a close similarity to the description of Esther's abortive attempt to drown herself during the picnic with Jody and her friends, and 'Man in Black' is another description of the area around Deer Island prison which Esther visits in an earlier attempt at suicide.

These poems, written between mid 1958 and autumn 1959, develop the sombre theme of the contrast between the fragile transience of man's experience and the obstinate survival of nature, which has appeared in poems such as 'Hardcastle Crags' and 'All the Dead Dears'. 'Two Views of a Cadaver Room' opposes the matter-of-fact acceptance of medical students dissecting corpses to the vision of Breughel, who saw love as a human force proof against the horror of the 'carrion army' even though it cannot withstand the 'death's head' which it disregards. The poet's own despondency is modified by an acceptance of the power of a love which persists despite its apparent fragility:

> These Flemish lovers flourish; not for long.

> Yet desolation, stalled in paint, spares the little country
> Foolish, delicate, in the lower right hand corner.

This dependency on the power of love as a justification of existence, even of suffering, is replaced in *Ariel* by the cynical disillusion of 'The Applicant': 'My boy, it's your last resort./Will you marry it, marry it, marry it', or 'The Couriers': 'A ring of gold with the sun in it?/Lies. Lies and a grief.'

'Point Shirley' translates the tragic theme of the impermanence of the human experience from the general to the particular in a reflection on the poet's own grandmother, prompted, presumably, by Sylvia Plath's visit to the house which had so gallantly withstood the 1938 hurricane. Although the house itself still stands firm against the steadily encroaching sea the grandmother is dead and all the poet's desire to recapture and remember the dead woman's spirit serves only to intensify her desolate sense of the hostility of the natural world, here symbolised in the predatory sea:

25

> A labour of love, and that labour lost.
> Steadily the sea
> Eats at Point Shirley. She died blessed,
> And I come by
> Bones, bones only, pawed and tossed,
> A dog-faced sea.

It was during this year that Sylvia Plath began to attend Robert Lowell's poetry classes held at Boston University and Ted Hughes has said that 'Point Shirley' is a 'deliberate exercise in Robert Lowell's early style'.[7] The conception of a sea which has the savagery and rapacity of a beast as it claws at the New England coast is reminiscent of the finest of Lowell's early poems, 'The Quaker Graveyard in Nantucket', while the nostalgic reflections on a dead grandparent are similar in mood to Lowell's elegies for his grandparents: 'In Memory of Arthur Winslow' and 'Mary Winslow'. Sylvia Plath explicitly indicated her admiration for Robert Lowell's later work, but the evidence of this poem suggests that she had also been impressed by the metaphoric vigour and verbal density of his earlier poetry, and it is hardly surprising that at a time when she was attending Lowell's poetry classes and was living in that area of Boston that is also Lowell's native environment that she should turn to his work. It may not be entirely coincidental that in another poem of this period, 'Suicide Off Egg Rock', she uses the word 'spindrift' which Lowell had used in the first line of his poem 'Salem': 'In Salem seasick spindrift drifts or skips'.

The sea opposes itself to the human struggle in 'Point Shirley', but in 'Suicide Off Egg Rock' it offers the only calm haven to the man who is tortured by his minutely detailed awareness of the sordid, man-made desert of the modern industrial society. In such a landscape he views his body as no more than 'A machine to breathe and beat forever', giving him unwilling existence in a life which oppresses him, although the prospect of the physical decay of death also disturbs him as he watches it exemplified in the flies penetrating the body of a dead fish. The only escape from so bleak a vision must be into the oblivion of death, and the sound of the sea as he enters it and 'The forgetful surf

7. *Ibid.*, p. 191.

creaming on those ledges' becomes the only pleasant element in the scene.

'The Hermit at Outermost House' returns to the theme in 'Point Shirley' of the hostility of the elements towards the human being, but suggests that by withstanding this hostility man may eventually defeat it, not through any conventional stance of thought or feeling but by the formulation of an obscure mystical insight, expressed by the poet as a 'certain meaning green'. A similar sense informs 'Man in Black' which places a human figure, even though rather sinisterly clothed in 'dead/Black', as the central feature which dominates and welds together the non-human elements of prison, domestic animals, sea, cliffs and break-water. The poem is basically visual; the poet forces the reader as the painter forces his audience, to see the scene with her eyes.

'Aftermath', another poem of this third group, turns from a con-sideration of the relationship between elements and man to scrutinise the terrible, obsessive fascination which human suffer-ing has for the onlooker, who is excited vicariously without the pain of involvement. The reference to 'Mother Medea' may seem over-literary, but the figures of Greek mythology appear quite frequently in Sylvia Plath's early poetry, fulfilling in a more muted way the function of the historical references of the later poetry, by providing concrete examples of pain against which the personal experience of the poet can be projected. The greater suffering of the 'austere tragedies' has been replaced in 'After-math' by a much more commonplace disaster which, because it does not involve death, scandal or great injury, disappoints the watching crowd. In a later poem, 'Lady Lazarus', Sylvia Plath was to cry out even more bitterly against the brutal indifference of the modern crowd to the sufferings of others. The subject of the later poem suggests that 'Aftermath' may also have been occa-sioned by her memories of the reactions of others to her suicide attempt and nervous breakdown at nineteen. Ted Hughes has said of 'Aftermath', 'Two Views of a Cadaver Room' and 'Suicide Off Egg Rock':[8] 'they steer in quite masterfully towards some point in her life that had been painful. For the first time she tried deliberately to locate just what it was that hurt'. The personal details are well-hidden in these early poems, but in this third

8. *Ibid.*, p. 191.

group it is possible to detect a new insistence on personal experience which was to develop into the openly autobiographical poems of the later period.

Particularly noteworthy in this respect are two of the strangest poems in *The Colossus*: the title poem and 'The Beekeeper's Daughter', of which Ted Hughes has somewhat enigmatically written:[9]

> 'The Beekeeper's Daughter' is one of a group of poems that she wrote at this time about her father . . . This poem, one of her chilliest, recounts a key event in her Viva Nuova.

The poem is chiefly effective as a very sensuous evocation of a specific moment in a garden which has darker undertones for the daughter of the title. The great profusion and fertility of the garden menaces the girl with a suffocating and encroaching richness, concentrated in her awareness of the strong colours of the flowers—purple, scarlet, orange, red—and their scents which are 'almost too dense to breathe in'. With a silent and deliberate wantonnness the flowers are opening themselves for fertilisation, which is described in human and royal terms. Through this scene moves the beekeeper with old-fashioned majesty; he is seen as the priestly lord of the bees and also of his daughter, who feels that her love for him is a subjection of self: 'My heart under your foot, sister of a stone', but at the end of the second verse she hints that in the luxuriant sexuality of such a setting she will supplant her mother, becoming the queen to the 'maestro of the bees'. In the final verse this hint is elaborated:

> Father, bridegroom, in this Easter egg
> Under the coronal of sugar roses
>
> The queen bee marries the winter of your year.

In 'Electra on Azalea Path',[10] an uncollected poem of the same time, the exultancy of this conclusion has been replaced by des-

9. *Ibid.*, p. 190.
10. 'Electra on Azalea Path', *op. cit.*

28

pairing guilt as the girl, caught in a welter of emotions, feels that her love was the cause of her father's death:

> Oh pardon the one who knocks for pardon at
> Your gate, father—your hound-bitch, daughter, friend.
> It was my love that did us both to death.

In 'Daddy' Sylvia Plath was to write an even more explicit and powerful poem about the relationship between daughter and father which contained both desire and fear, affection and the urge to destroy. In 'Daddy' she addresses the dead father in the following way: 'Ghastly statue with one grey toe/Big as a Frisco seal', and this image recalls the title-poem of the earlier volume in which the father–daughter relationship is treated through the medium of an archeological metaphor. As in 'The Beekeeper's Daughter' the meaning of the poem lies not on the surface but through the accumulation of allusions and suggestions. The image of the devotion of great effort to the cleansing and repairing of a massive statue, a task which has already occupied thirty years yet seems no nearer completion, and which engrosses and subjugates the persona, whose humorous derision is underlain by a total commitment to her task, is fascinating and powerful in itself. However it seems impossible to separate meaning and metaphor without doing the poem a serious injustice for its essence lies in the skilfully maintained balance between the concrete situation with its appropriate visual details and the relation of these details to the underlying emotion. The last three lines of the poem, for instance, contain much more than a particularly striking image:

> My hours are married to shadow.
> No longer do I listen for the scrape of a keel
> On the blank stones of the landing.

This final image has considerable pathos and beauty and is imaginatively in unity with the growing despair of the earlier verses, but read in conjunction with the line which immediately precedes it, it is also a statement of the submission of the restorer to the broken statue and her acceptance, indicated in the word

29

'married', that there can be no escape from this memory into a more vital relationship. In such a life everything must be shadowy, blank, lonely, but she accepts her isolation almost with fervour.

'The Colossus' has the direct, conversational tone of the later poems and it is written in the five-line verse which Sylvia Plath was to use most consistently in *Ariel*, in fourteen out of the forty poems, although in this first volume only six poems have five-lined verses. The earlier tendency to choose the esoteric or archaic word has now disappeared, although the rather unusual 'skull-plates' is also used in another poem of this group, 'Two Views of a Cadaver Room'. The verses are not rhymed and the line lengths follow no regular pattern; the poem is by no means formless but is much less strictly and rigidly controlled than those poems written two years earlier. In this greater elasticity can be seen the forerunner of Sylvia Plath's later style which she admitted was much closer to the rhythms of spoken English than that of her earlier poetry:[11]

> This is something I didn't do in my earlier poems. For
> example, my first book, *The Colossus*, I can't read any
> of the poems aloud now. I didn't write them to be read
> aloud. They, in fact, quite privately bore me. These
> ones that I have just read, the ones that are most
> recent, I've got to say them, I speak them to myself,
> and I think that this in my own writing development is
> quite a new thing with me, and whatever lucidity they
> may have comes from the fact that I say them to
> myself, I say them aloud.

The fourth and final group of poems in this volume, written during the weeks spent at Yaddo, have—with the exception of 'Poem for a Birthday'—an external and meditative focus which is in contrast to the poems of 1958-9 which form a series of personal explorations. The poet projects herself into the poems of this final group not as a specific individual with a unique existence, but as one member of a humanity unified by the common demands of existence. The vision is less bleak than that of the earlier poems because the focus has been widened into a conception of a systematically similar experience which includes the human world, the

11. Orr, *op. cit.*, p. 170.

animal and the vegetable. The emphasis is now placed on the common mutability and on the inevitable outcome of the struggle between actuality and desire in a life described in 'The Burnt-Out Spa' as a fast-flowing stream which 'Neither nourishes nor heals'.

'The Manor Garden' concentrates on the autumnal decay of a formal garden which is almost certainly that of Yaddo, and which is probably also the subject of the poem 'Private Ground', published two years later. The imminent arrival of an entity to whom the poet addresses herself at times directly, at times obliquely as she muses on her surroundings, counterpoints the sadness involved in the dying year. Sylvia Plath's first child was born on 1 April 1960, and it seems not unlikely that during the weeks at Yaddo her pregnancy increased her awareness of the cycle of birth and death which is endlessly repetitive and which would affect her unborn child as herself. Certainly the first two verses of the poem are clearer in meaning if the poem is addressed to a foetus. The development of the foetus from its resemblance to a fish to its resemblance to a pig matches the decay and death of the natural world, which will, also, in time bring forth new life. The last two lines of the poem are crucial in uniting the perceptions of the external world of the garden with the thoughts of the unborn child and express the culmination of the poem's mood of mingled joy and sadness: 'The small birds converge, converge/With their gifts to a difficult borning.'

'Mushrooms' employs images of organic growth and development but its implications are altogether darker and more sinister than those of 'The Manor Garden'. Ted Hughes explains[12] that the poem was the result of a series of invocations and meditative exercises which he and Sylvia Plath devised together during their time at Yaddo. The poem describes the sinister, silent mass movement of mushrooms as they push upwards through the ground. The sense that the mushrooms will eventually take over the world relates the poem to 'The Thin People', an even more chilling poem of the second group, which pictures the submission of the vitality of the world to the calm, indifferent encroachment of the forces of lethargy and spiritual blankness which must triumph merely by existing. At this point in her poetic development the poet expresses feeling through the minutely detailed description

12. Hughes, *op. cit.*, p. 191.

of objects. It is only in the final poem of this volume that she abandons this restraint of both emotion and form and begins a more nakedly direct self-exploration.

All the poems of *The Colossus* are accomplished, but the major achievement, because it indicates such a radical change in attitude and intention, is the series of poems which form 'Poem For a Birthday'. Ted Hughes has written of this series:[13]

> She was reading Paul Radin's collection of African folktales with great excitement. In these she found the underworld of her worst nightmares throwing up intensely beautiful adventures, where the most unsuspected voices thrived under the pressures of a reality that made most accepted fiction seem artificial and spurious. At the same time she was reading— closely and sympathetically for the first time— Roethke's poems. The result was a series of pieces, each a monologue of some character in an underground, primitive drama.

These pieces, with the exception of the final one, are very similar in subject and imagery to some of Roethke's poetry and suggest his influence in their insistence on the insect and vegetable world. Formally 'Poem For a Birthday' is also reminiscent of Roethke's work, particularly of the poems he collected in *Praise to the End*,[14] in the division of the poem into separate sections connected by dominant themes and imagery. The short, sharp, frequently end-stopped lines give an effect of jerky and painful communication in both 'Poem For a Birthday' and *Praise to the End*.

The first section of 'Poem For a Birthday' is entitled 'Who'. Four strands can be detected in this first section: references to the poet's pregnancy, memories of her experiences in the mental hospital, descriptions of her surroundings at Yaddo and the use of typically Roethkean imagery to describe states of mind. The title of the whole poem suggests that it was written in October, the month of Sylvia Plath's birthday, and the third line of the first verse reinforces this by referring to October. The opening images

13. *Ibid.*, p. 192.
14. *Praise to The End*, 1951. *Collected Poems*, Faber, 1968, pp. 71–92.

of autumnal harvesting and storing for the winter also have reference to the poet's own condition of pregnancy and the line: 'This shed's fusty as a mummy's stomach' is probably deliberately ambiguous; the primary reference to the Egyptian mummy which encloses the dead body is underscored by a reference to the womb which houses and protects the unborn child. Throughout the poem images of death and birth are combined in this way. The total experience of the first section is one of death and dullness; the persona longs to immerse her identity in her natural surroundings, to become so minute a part of the potting shed setting that even 'The spiders won't notice'. The potting shed is filled with old, unused, decaying, rusty objects which fascinate the poet because they are cast aside and unused. If she becomes a part of such a scene then she will be able to renounce all calls on herself and sink back into a state of utter nullity. Ultimately she longs for death as a state of complete repose which could be achieved if life would cease its insistent demands: 'If only the wind would leave my lungs alone'.

The second part of 'Who' suddenly turns from the potting shed and references to approaching maternity to the mental hospital, but the reader used to the sudden transitions of Roethke's poems accepts this easily. The experience of mental illness has been one of complete loss of identity, of a feeling of being one with inanimate nature: 'I am a root, a stone, an owl pellet,/Without dreams of any sort.' The poet has welcomed this self-immolation and has longed for the further silences of death which she glimpses lurking behind the world of objects; death is seen as a mother who devours her offspring, but to whom the persona longs to succumb. The experience of mental disintegration has not been an altogether ugly one, it has a weird beauty of its own generated by the poet's feelings of smallness and insignificance which cause her to see her surroundings with heightened perceptiveness: 'There were such enormous flower,/Purple and red mouths, utterly lovely.' The note on which this section ends is less successful because it moves from the Roethkean world of animal and vegetable imagery to a closer approximation to a more mundane world: 'Now they light me up like an electric bulb./For weeks I can remember nothing at all.' The simile of the electric bulb is too forcedly ingenious and too determinedly shocking to be totally successful, although the final bleak references to the loss of memory which often follows electro-convulsive therapy are chilling.

The influence of Roethke on 'Poem For a Birthday' can be found most obviously in the second section of the poem, 'Dark House'. Sylvia Plath's 'I am round as an owl,/I see by my own light' has the same cadence as Roethke's 'I'm an otter with only one nose:/I'm all ready to whistle'[15] as well as the same technique of identification with the animal world. 'Any day I may litter puppies/Or mother a horse'. 'My belly moves' is a reference to Sylvia Plath's pregnancy but it also recalls the perverted fertility of Roethke's 'Sit and play/Under the rocker/Until the cows/All have puppies'.[16] The subterranean animal inhabitant of 'Dark House', eating its way to a final depth in the bowel of the root, is associated with images of the womb and is significantly 'Moley-handed'; in Roethke's poem 'The Lost Son'[17] it is the mole who leads him to the 'slime of a wet nest', also associated with images of the womb and birth. Throughout 'Dark House' the movements of the strange, underground animal are linked with the pre-birth stirrings of the developing child. A deeper but more central refer-ence is to the attempt of the questing mind to build a security from the depths of self: 'This is a dark house, very big./I made it myself,/Cell by cell from a quiet corner.' However the quest for knowledge leads only to an acceptance of the comfort of escape:

> It is warm and tolerable
> In the bowel of the root.
> Here's a cuddly mother.

The third section of Sylvia Plath's poem, 'Maenad', is central. The poet returns to memories of childhood, which she sees as a time when she was not differentiated from others as she is now, when she lived in a safe world under the guardianship of an omnipotent father:

> Once I was ordinary:
> Sat by my father's bean tree
> Eating the fingers of wisdom.

15. 'O Lull Me, Lull Me', *Collected Poems*, pp. 83–4.
16. 'Where Knock Is Open Wide', *Ibid.*, pp. 71–4.
17. *Ibid.*, pp. 53–8.

But when the father died the conflict between child and mother disrupted the harmony of the world; in any case time has irretrievably divided the adult from the child's world of innocence and the earlier symbols are now meaningless: 'Birdmilk is feathers,/The bean leaves are dumb as hands.' The only way to overcome the childhood conflicts is to repulse them by evolving a new identity, and the mother, the dominant, oppressive figure in these conflicts, must also be repulsed: 'Mother, keep out of my barnyard,/I am becoming another.' The end of the quest must lie in acceptance of the whole personality and Sylvia Plath's 'I am becoming another' is strongly reminiscent of Roethke's: 'I'm somebody else now.'[18] One escape from the anguish of the struggle to recognise self can be found in the silence of death and this is still longed for but cannot be achieved, so the wearying, unrolling procession of time must be endured. The section ends with a statement of the complete loss of identity and individuality, but one slight note of hope is now introduced for the persona is actively seeking a name which will define her personality: 'Tell me my name.' The questioning, insistent and repeated, of some outside entity forms a recurrent feature of Roethke's poetry, thus: 'Have I come to always?', 'How high is have?', 'Can I have my heart back?'

'The Beast', the fourth section of the poem, develops the opposition between childhood, when the girl was happy and secure guarded by her father's love, and the present situation of spiritual loss and desolation. Nothing could go wrong in her father's reign, for he was all-powerful: 'Breathing was easy in his airy holding./ The sun sat in his armpit', but now the father has deserted his daughter who finds herself wandering, lost and abandoned in the deepest recesses of some underground kingdom of despair: 'I housekeep in Time's gut-end/Among emmets and molluscs,/Duchess of Nothing,/Hairtusk's bride'. The description of the father as 'King of the dish, my lucky animal' brings to mind the disturbingly repellent opening of Roethke's 'I Need, I Need':[19] 'A deep dish. Lumps in it./I can't taste my mother.' An obscure note of sexuality which combines both fascination and revulsion appears in the work of both poets.

18. 'Where Knock is Open Wide', *op. cit.*
19. *Ibid.*, pp. 74-7.

The fifth section of 'Poem For a Birthday', 'Flute Notes From a Reedy Pond', indicates the influence of Roethke's poetry less clearly than the previous sections. The short, choppy lines have given way to a longer, smoother, more lyrical line. The poem now begins to move towards its tentative conclusion, and the end of Sylvia Plath's quest differs from the end of Roethke's. Thus the imagery and rhythm are beginning to diverge. The world evoked is one of coldness, laziness, blankness and the protagonist is some minute fish or insect living on the bed of a lily pond. The general conception of the scene is Roethkean, but the restless energy of the earlier stanzas has become the slower reflectiveness of: 'Hourly the eye of the sky enlarges its blank/Dominion. The stars are no nearer.' The persona feels that she has reached a state of complete nullity, secure even from tension and obsession: 'This is not death, it is something safer./The wingy myths won't tug at us any more.' This fifth section marks a point of unresolved stasis in the poem, for the sixth section, 'Witchburning', returns to the restlessness of the earlier parts, although the energy is now directed wholly towards recovery and the discovery of a birthday. The lines are still longer than in sections one to four, but the tone becomes conversational again. The persona realises that she is both tormented and tormenting and the only escape from such a condition is to live through the exorcism of it for only 'the devil can eat the devil out'. The protagonist has finally accepted that the condition of her illness is one in which she is both the witch and the wax doll, the persecutor and the persecuted. In this month of her birthday she has begun to accept the recovery of psychic identity and wholeness. She acknowledges that it is too easy to blame the powers of sickness and yet remain in the sick state, the return to health will be a painful process of growth and development from which there will be no easy escape: 'It hurts at first. The red tongues will teach the truth.'

Roethke's quest most characteristically ends in a moment of revelation which quickly falls back into the old state of waiting, or in a pantheistic statement of considerable beauty. Sylvia Plath's ends on a much bleaker note and employs imagery alien to Roethke's poetry. The seventh section of 'Poem For a Birthday', 'The Stones', is a description of the return to sanity, not in the terms of the ecstatic if painful exorcism of 'Witchburning', but with the clinical and technical imagery of surgery and spare parts. The recovery of health is not, as in Roethke's poetry, an organic awareness of wholeness, but a patching or repairing process. The persona no longer takes an active part in this process, she becomes a body worked on by cheerful if impersonal doctors:

> The grafters are cheerful,
>
> Heating the pincers, hoisting the delicate hammers.
> A current agitates the wires
> Volt upon volt. Catgut stitches my fissures.

This imagery of mechanical parts and surgery appears in Sylvia Plath's later poetry also and it is integrally connected with the experience of recovery from mental disturbance. She associates the curative process with love, but love is an ambiguous force which can combine both affection and menace: 'Love is the uniform of my bald nurse./Love is the bone and sinew of my curse.' The image of recovery in terms of a rose held in a vase: 'The vase, reconstructed, houses/The elusive rose' is the only faint echo of Roethke. It may bear some relation to his:[20]

> To know that light falls and fills, often without our
>   knowing,
> As an opaque vase fills to the brim from a quick
>   pouring,
> Fills and trembles at the edge yet does not flow over,
> Still holding and feeding the stem of the contained
>   flower.

However Sylvia Plath's poem does not end on a lyrical note, the final image suggests sterility and smallness: 'Ten fingers shape a bowl for shadows./My mendings itch. There is nothing to do./I shall be as good as new.' The feeling is similar to that Lowell records at the end of 'Home After Three Months Away':[20] 'Cured, I am frizzled, stale and small.'

The influence of Roethke on Sylvia Plath can be confined to the

20. 'The Shape of the Fire', *Ibid.*, pp. 64–7.
21. *Life Studies*, Faber, 1959, p. 55.

earlier stanzas of this one long poem. She encountered Roethke's strange, individual, troubled poetry at an important point in her development. The menace of her own work was becoming a more and more insistent element, and a sympathetic study of Roethke's poetry showed her how to allow the sinister elements to rise to the surface of the poem without overwhelming it. Under his influence she was able to discard the formality and restraint of her earlier poetry in favour of this much freer, more immediate work. Most of the poems collected in *The Colossus* are nature poems, in the sense that the imagery is drawn from the poet's apprehension of the natural world, and many of the poems are concerned with evaluating and defining the relationship between the poet and the outside world. In 'Poem For a Birthday' she was able for the first time to complete the process of fusion between internal preoccupations and outer perceptions. The influence of Roethke in showing her that it was possible to do this, and that the most intimate of subjects could become subjects for poetry, is more important than the purely verbal and rhythmic influences which can be found in 'Poem For a Birthday'. Thematically and stylistically this last poem is much closer to the more relaxed later work than to the exploratory discipline of the earlier volume. It heralds her major work and is in itself a considerable achievement.

3 *Crossing the Water*

Seen from the perspective of *Ariel The Colossus* has usually been defined and judged as a starting point, in fact it more properly represents the final stage in the first phase of Sylvia Plath's work. She had been publishing poems fairly regularly. in the late fifties and Ted Hughes has pointed out that she scrapped many poems before *The Colossus* took its final shape.[1] The real starting point of the final development can be found in the poems now collected in *Crossing the Water*, although it is hinted at in 'Poem For a Birthday', the last and in many ways the most untypical poem in *The Colossus*. Many of these poems were first published in journals and magazines in 1961 and 1962; 'Candles'[2] in fact was published as early as November 1960. *The Colossus* was submitted to Heinemann at the end of January 1960; *Winter Trees* and *Ariel* largely represent the work of the last year of her life, so it seems that the transitional phase from *The Colossus* to *Ariel* lasted from late 1959 when she wrote 'Poem For a Birthday', to early 1962. During this time the Hughes returned to England, moved from London to Devon, had two children and *Crossing the Water* reflects these events, although its major exploration is an internal one.

Two of the poems in *Crossing the Water*, 'I Am Vertical' and 'Private Ground', overlap in subject and mood with the last group of poems in *The Colossus*. 'Private Ground' was first published in *Critical Quarterly*[3] a year later than 'The Manor Garden', which also describes the grounds at Yaddo. Its mood is less equivocal than that of 'The Manor Garden', although it is informed by the same brooding melancholy, which has not yet darkened into the depression of many of the poems of 1962 and 1963. The poem establishes a state of regression and self-enclosure; everything is

---

1. Hughes, *op. cit.*, p. 188.
2. 'Candles', *The Listener*, lxiv, 17 November 1960, p. 877.
3. 'Private Ground', *Critical Quarterly*, 3, Summer 1961, p. 140.

being packed away, cleared up, drained for the approaching rigours of winter. The boundary wall itself, in protecting the estate from the outer world, represented by the ceaseless flow of traffic on the highway beyond, also encloses and to some extent imprisons it. The estate serves as a reminder of an older, calmer if declining civilisation for the owner had ornamented the grounds with statues brought from 'Europe's relic heap'. Yet the estate gradually changes its identity with the arrival of the early frosts, even the day 'forgets itself'. Although the poet is saddened by this regression it cannot calm her, for her consciousness becomes the medium which focuses all the different impressions. We are still recognisably in the world of *The Colossus* with its clear visual annotations and descriptions, but a new seriousness has entered the poem. The private world of the estate encourages the poet's introverted melancholy; she becomes increasingly aware of pain as well as beauty. She makes the gesture of rescuing the fish left to die on the basin of the drained pond, but has no option to give, for the lake she transfers them to is itself a forbidding haven;

> Morgue of old logs and old images, the lake
> Opens and shuts, accepting them among its reflections.

In 'I Am Vertical' Sylvia Plath sees herself as irrevocably separated from the nature which she admires and envies. Only death will bring her into a meaningful relationship with the trees and flowers which she enjoys because they represent for her qualities she lacks. She has neither the tree's sturdy life nor the flower's more transient beauty: 'And I want the one's longevity and the other's daring.' The poem reveals the same ability to talk about death simply, lyrically and without any sign of the usual urgency or pain which can be found in the very late poems. Its understated delicacy provides an effective contrast to the searing vitality of 'Fever 103°' or 'Lady Lazarus', yet its calm decisiveness is equally striking. She makes explicit in this poem the reference to death which was constantly hinted at in *The Colossus*:

> It is more natural to me, lying down.
> Then the sky and I are in open conversation,
> And I shall be useful when I lie down finally:

> Then the tree may touch me for once, and the
> flowers have time for me.

Five of the poems in *Crossing the Water* record Sylvia Plath's reactions to particular places, two to the USA and three to England. They are 'Sleep in the Mojave Desert', 'Two Campers in Cloud Country' and 'Wuthering Heights', 'Finisterre', 'Parliament Hill Fields' respectively. The first two seem likely to be memories of the camping holiday spent by the Hughes in 1959 which culminated in their stay at Yaddo. 'Two Campers in Cloud Country', which is subtitled 'Rock Lake, Canada', reveals Sylvia Plath's feelings not only about her native Boston but also about America generally. The campers flee from Boston in protest against its fastidiously organised politeness; they want a larger, more assertive landscape where nature and not man is dominant. They arrive at 'the last frontiers of the big, brash spirit' and at first are delighted by the empty spaciousness which represents the more active aspect of America's heritage. Gradually however this becomes faintly menacing: history has not affected this vastness, America's troubled past, which seemed such a guarantee of solidity, is wiped out: 'The Pilgrims and Indians might never have happened.' Sylvia Plath is not content with a mere description of her reactions to Rock Lake in this poem, she also states one of her recurrent themes, that of the frailty of the individual's sense of self, which was stifled by Boston's prettiness, but is even more seriously threatened by the open spaces it sought:

> Around our tent the old simplicities sough
> Sleepily as Lethe, trying to get in.
> We'll wake blank-brained as water in the dawn.

It was not just in America that she felt that landscape threatened her; at 'Finisterre' also she feels effaced, silenced, neutralised: 'I walk among them, and they stuff my mouth with cotton.' The visual apprehension of the painter creates the opening image of the poem as she sees the end of the land as a great, black hand, 'Cramped on nothing'. Greatness, even though frequently destructive and terrifying, belongs to the past, the present is 'only gloomy'. The description of 'Our Lady of the Shipwrecked' in the third verse deliberately echoes Lowell's 'Our Lady of Walsing-ham',[4] the sixth section of his 'Quaker Graveyard in Nantucket'. As in Lowell's poem the Lady's face expresses nothing, but where-as Lowell's Lady's neutrality was the only possible expression of a Divinity beyond human conception, Sylvia Plath's Lady is supremely unaware of the human figures praying to her for, 'She is in love with the beautiful formlessness of the sea'. The poem ends with a vision of a different sea, one which produces shells to be made into pretty trivialities; a sea which is quite different from 'the Bay of the Dead down there', but it is the latter which engages Sylvia Plath's imagination.

The vast expanses of uncivilised nature are again seen as more powerful than all the fortifications of structured society in 'Wuthering Heights'. Although written after 'Hardcastle Crags' it can, in some ways, be seen as a companion poem to it. Like 'Hardcastle Crags' 'Wuthering Heights' analyses a response to the bleak landscape of West Yorkshire, however the strongly expressed feeling of personal isolation which pervades the poem is closer to the mood of 'Sheep in Fog'. Throughout *Ariel* the poet searches for warmth in the vibrant red of poppies and roses, in the innocence of children, in the normality of human gestures, but the colours of the poems are gradually reduced to black and white, the world becomes colder and greyer. In 'Wuthering Heights' also the elusive, indefinable promise of the distance always evades her as she moves eagerly towards it. Only the sky offers any solidity or stability and even this hope is undermined by the evocation of paleness and neutrality. She moves hopefully towards a horizon which is itself unstable and which never fulfils its promise of warmth:

> The horizons ring me like faggots,
> Tilted and disparate, and always unstable.
> Touched by a match, they might warm me,
> And their fine lines singe
> The air to orange
> Before the distances they pin evaporate,
> Weighting the pale sky with a solider colour.

4. 'The Quaker Graveyard in Nantucket', *Poems 1938–1949*, Faber, 1960, p. 18.

But they only dissolve and dissolve
Like a series of promises, as I step forward.

The high, moorland landscape represents a serious threat for it tries with its windy coldness to draw from her the little heat and life she still retains. As in 'Hardcastle Crags' she feels herself to be physically vulnerable in such a stony, unyielding landscape. The sheep are happier and luckier than she is for they 'know what they are' and their unblinking stare further reduces her self-confidence until she becomes a letter 'mailed into space'. This sense of oneself as inanimate becomes more common in *Ariel*, perhaps it finds its clearest expression in 'Cut': 'I have taken a pill to kill/The thin Papery feeling.' It also appears in *Crossing the Water*, particularly in the title poem where the voyagers over the water are 'two black cut-paper people'. This phrase occurs again in 'Tulips', where Sylvia Plath conveys the depression and lethargy following illness in her description of herself as a 'cut-paper shadow'. The combination of blackness, shadow, paper in these images is a powerful expression of the constant feeling of a lack of reality, a substance-lessness which pervades the later work. She is still capable, however, of considerable objective humour, the despondency of her vision in 'Wuthering Heights' is highlighted by her picture of the sheep as rather foolish elderly ladies:

> They stand about in grandmotherly disguise,
> All wig curls and yellow teeth
> And hard, marbly baas.

As she walks on across the moor she feels herself to be exploring an unpeopled landscape very similar to the empty spaces of 'Two Campers in Cloud Country'. The black stoniness which depressed her in 'Hardcastle Crags' is also dominant here and she wants ultimately to become a part of this scene, for she sees herself as too obtrusive because she is 'the one upright/Among all horizontals'. She identifies herself with the grass in its terrified revolt against impenetrable blackness, but looking back to the human communities in the distant valleys she finds no suggestion of escape or peace there, for they are mean and self-enclosed. Although they both wrote of extremes of feeling Sylvia Plath has little in

43

common with Emily Brontë who saw this wild landscape as a source of exultancy; to Sylvia Plath it represents the death of the self.

'Parliament Hill Fields', first published in August, 1961,[5] describes a quite different landscape. It seems to have reference to the miscarriage which Sylvia Plath experienced in the winter of 1960–1. In this poem the apparent rejection of the woman by the landscape is a reflection of her inner loss, but the introversion of grief doesn't hinder her eye from brilliantly perceiving the visual effects: 'the city melts like sugar'. Just as she is rejected by the landscape she also feels herself to be rejected by people; the school-girls disregard her, confirming her conception of her own utter unimportance: 'I'm a stone, a stick'. The imagery of bareness, deprivation, infertility subtly establishes the mood of withdrawal. The only offer made to her by the landscape is that of the silent forgetfulness of death but the poem refuses all self-indulgence by finally admitting the transience of grief and reasserting the desire for life. She returns to the living child, safe and warm in the nursery, relinquishing her grief for the dead one. However, this recovery allows all the old ambivalences to flood back again; the division between the bright warmth of the house and the cold half-light outside is a far from absolute one:

> The old dregs, the old difficulties take me to wife.
> Gulls stiffen to their chilld vigil in the draughty half-
> light;
> I enter the lit house.

There are several images associated with illness in 'Parliament Hill Fields'. The flock of gulls flying inland reminds her of an invalid's hands, the wind is like a bandage, Kentish Town is swaddled in white, the new moon is like the white, taut skin over a scar, the gulls 'stiffen' in the evening. This imagery of hospitals, illness, suffering can be identified as a constant characteristic of Sylvia Plath's work from 'Poem For a Birthday' onwards and it finds frequent expression in these transitional poems of *Crossing the Water*. The most obvious instance can be found in 'Surgeon at 2 a.m.' which reveals a fascination with various aspects of surgery

5. 'Parliament Hill Fields', *London Magazine*, 1 (n.s.), August 1961, p. 7.

and disease. The poem mirrors the tired surgeon's perception of the weird, surreal beauty of the body he operates on. The vivid colours, strong smells and rhythmic pulsing of the body's organs remind him of his own insignificance:

> It is a garden I have to do with—tubers and fruits
> Oozing their jammy substances,
> A mat of roots. My assistants hook them back.
> Stenches and colours assail me.
> This is the lung-tree.
> These orchids are splendid. They spot and coil like
> snakes.
> The heart is a red-bell-bloom, in distress.
> I am so small
> In comparison to these organs!

This sense of reverence and personal insignificance as he works with the garden and wilderness of the body is balanced by his acceptance of the patient's utter reliance on him. He sees himself walking through the ward in the early morning, watching over the patients who seem dead in their gauze wrappings and he accepts the responsibility of being the source of all their hopes: 'I am the sun in my white coat/Grey faces, shuttered by drugs, follow me like flowers.' At this stage Sylvia Plath writes of the doctor with considerable compassion and intuitive understanding; in *Ariel* she more bleakly associates the disease imagery with a depersonalised world of mechanised medicine; of spare parts and substitutes in 'The Applicant', of deformity, pain and ugly death in 'Berck-Plage'. The doctor of *Ariel* appears as the concentration camp experimenter of 'Lady Lazarus' rather than as the compassionate healer of 'Surgeon at 2 a.m.'.

Associated with the disease and illness imagery are the recurrent references to death which thread through *Crossing the Water*. In 'Small Hours', first published in August 1961,[6] Sylvia Plath again writes of the contrast between expectation and actuality which is one of the dominant themes of *The Colossus*. The persona sees herself as an empty but architecturally ornate museum, yearning for the magnificence of statues and fountains

6. 'Small Hours', *Ibid.*, p. 7.

which play constantly. Instead she is faced with a world of stulti-
fication and sterility in which her dreams of power and greatness
give way to the reality which surrounds her. She can find no possibility of advance or communication in this world, symbolised by
the lilies of death, watched over by the blankness of the moon: 'the
dead injure me with attentions, and nothing can happen.' The
imagery of the poem has clear associations with both earlier and
later work; the statues, pillars, porticoes are reminiscent of 'The
Colossus' and the references to Nike and Apollo are also a
reminder of the classical figures of the earlier volume. However
the central image is also linked to the similar image of 'Morning
Song': 'New statue./In a drafty museum, your nakedness/
Shadows our safety.' The sinister, neutral importance of the moon
is frequently echoed in the later poetry also. The feeling of helplessness and imprisonment characteristic of *The Bell Jar* also finds
expression here: 'nothing can happen'. She expresses the same
feeling later in 'The Moon and the Yew Tree': 'I simply cannot
see where there is to get to.' Inescapably Sylvia Plath is no longer
concerned, as she was in *The Colossus*, with the relationship
between the individual and his environment; her poems now
describe a subjective, inner world. As they withdraw into this
world the voice of the poet begins to speak with a new bleak
authority.

Increasingly she sees herself as an actor in a distanced drama in
which the dominant colours are black and white; the white of the
cruel moonlight and the black of the water of death, the night and
the loneliness of the isolated self. One of the later poems in the
volume, 'Event', describes the failing relationship between lovers
pushed apart by one's perception of a pain so ineradicable and
firmly based that, 'Love cannot come here'. The lovers lie
separated from each other, bathed in the moonlight but only
aware that it illuminates the rift between them. The child who
sleeps beside them makes demands they cannot satisfy and the
stars beyond the window are a reminder of a light which 'burns
and sickens'. Even in the morning their gestures cannot be honest
and generous, for the woman is constantly aware of the growing
distance between them and the sense of being mutilated by this
distance shapes her responses: 'The dark is melting. We touch like
cripples.' The poem illustrates Sylvia Plath's developing power to

structure her poems around plain, direct statements: 'I cannot see your eyes.' She is also developing the exquisite lyrical references to nature which relieve the prevailing darkness of *Winter Trees* and *Ariel*: 'Where apple bloom ices the night.'

The quiet, restrained melancholy of 'Event' reflects one of the two moods of the poems in this volume; the other is a much more active, demanding assault, verbal and visual as in 'Leaving Early', first published eighteen months earlier than 'Event' in August 1961.[7] The consciousness which created 'Leaving Early' is brilliantly alert, it catalogues, responds, reacts, rarely allowing itself any resting point. The vision of the poem is not always fully directed yet it is authentic: the force and appropriateness of the comparisons being particularly effective: 'Velvet pillows the colour of blood pudding', 'chrysanthemums the size/Of Holofernes' head'. 'Leaving Early' is very similar in tone and style to 'Poem For a Birthday'; both are part of an underground drama in which objects and things acquire a pressing, superhuman reality. In 'Leaving Early' the Lady has filled her room with vases of cut flowers which encroach on the room and become more than human in their assertive reality:

> The red geraniums I know.
> Friends, friends. They stink of armpits
> And the involved maladies of autumn,
> Musky as a lovebed the morning after.

Her painfully aware brilliance sees the flowers as alive and pressing in on her and this gives the first half of the poem considerable vitality but the ending resolves itself into a more muted melancholy; the flowers' assertive strength is opposed to the cold withdrawal of the human beings and the recurrent stone image of 'Poem For a Birthday' and *The Bell Jar* reappears, as does the questioning of identity and situation which also occurs in Roethke's poetry:

> We slept like stones. Lady, what am I doing
> With a lung full of dust and a tongue of wood,
> Knee-deep in the cold and swamped by flowers?

7. 'Leaving Early', *Ibid.*, p. 9.

In a later poem, 'Blackberrying', first published in September, 1962,[8] Sylvia Plath once more forces nature to assume an almost human significance. The poem begins simply as a description of a lane leading down to the sea, bordered by heavily laden blackberry thorns but all the details of the description are infused by a desperate yet unexplained sense of urgency. Everything is larger than life; the ripe, huge berries and the birds wheeling overhead, the stillness of the afternoon and the regular hooks of the blackberry bushes are menacing to the girl who picks mechanically on, moving down the lane towards the sea. The poem arouses a similar response to a slightly later poem, 'The Rabbit Catcher', in its suggestion of latent menace contained in a perfectly normal, almost idyllic scene. The sea in 'Blackberrying' is, 'the only thing to come to' and yet when the lane ends and the poet finds herself faced by the open sea she can recognise it only as a further assault on her precarious sense of identity. The hooks of the blackberries have lured her on to this terrible noisy nothingness:

> . . . . A last hook brings me
> To the hills' northern face, and the face is orange rock
> That looks out on nothing, nothing but a great space
> Of white and pewter lights, and a din like silversmiths
> Beating and beating at an intractable metal.

Crossing the Water constantly confronts the known and normal with the unknown and terrible. In 'Pheasant', one of the few happy poems in the volume, Sylvia Plath rejoices in the pleasure which the pheasant's beauty brings into her world. An earlier poem about a bird, 'Black Rook in Rainy Weather', developed into an analysis of the nature of poetic inspiration; in 'Pheasant' the poet is content to see the bird as it is; she appreciates its solid yet rare reality; it remains simply itself and in doing so extends her own precariously maintained sense of self:

> I am not mystical: it isn't
> As if I thought it had a spirit.
> It is simply in its element.

8. 'Blackberrying', *The New Yorker*, xxxviii, 15 September 1962, p. 48.

48

These moments of calmness are few in *Crossing the Water*; much more typical is 'Apprehensions' which attempts to define the fears and pressures of the mind in terms of differently coloured, imprisoning walls—white, grey, red, black—the dominant colours of the later poetry. The intensity of the suffering increases as the colour of the wall changes. White represents a static indifference, an isolation which has the spurious peace of complete neutrality; the grey wall of the second verse is 'clawed and bloody' as a result of her attempts to break free; before her stands the wall, behind her steps lead down into deeper silence. This world is similar to that of the enclosing prison of the bell jar, the air of both is fetid and sour. The red wall of the third verse represents the muscular contractions of the heart automatically controlling the movement of the lungs; but behind the pain of living lurks the sharper fear of death: 'a terror/Of being wheeled off under crosses and a rain of pietas'. It is only in the poems written in the last few days of her life that Sylvia Plath consistently wrote of death without ambivalence. The final wall, an impenetrable black, represents a world of absolutes where there are neither dilemmas nor acceptances: 'Cold blanks approach us:/They move in a hurry.' This description is a premonition of the black resolution of the poems written in February, 1963.

Interviewed by Peter Orr, Sylvia Plath once said[9] that as a woman she felt that the world of domestic objects was particularly important to her. She expresses this idea in *Crossing the Water*, notably in 'Last Words' where she describes the coffin and burial she would like to have. In this poem, as in 'Mirror', the mirror is a symbol of a life which is drawing to an end, but the persona feels that death is a ceremony which should be attended by bravery and beauty, the dignified, plain coffin is not for her:

> I do not want a plain box, I want a sarcophagus
> With tigery stripes, and a face on it
> Round as the moon, to stare up.

The world of the spirit and the emotions threatens her because it is confusing and elusive, but objects and possessions have a comforting solidity. Long after the death of emotion loved objects will retain their associative power:

9. Orr, *op. cit.*, p. 171.

When the soles of my feet grow cold,
The blue eye of my turquoise will comfort me.
Let me have my copper cooking pots, let my rouge pots
Bloom about me like night flowers, with a good smell.

Sylvia Plath's own assessment of some of the poems she wrote during this transitional stage is a harsh one: 'These poems do not live: it's a sad diagnosis' she writes in 'Stillborn'. Certainly this volume is an uneven one, many of the poems succeeding brilliantly, a few failing, either because they are too esoteric in reference or because they are occasional pieces, extraneous to the developing opus with its complex but unified references and associations. As an experimental, transitional volume *Crossing the Water* is very valuable as a bridge between the early composure of *The Colossus* and the later originality and daring of *Ariel*. The poems represent Sylvia Plath's growing recognition and expression of her poetic subject, even though she felt in 'Stillborn' that some of the poems of this period were opaque: 'But they are dead, and their mother near dead with distraction,/And they stupidly stare, and do not speak of her.' This is merely the dissatisfaction of an artist developing so rapidly and basically that she constantly seeks new modes of expression. *Crossing the Water* looks forward to and often equals the achievement of *Ariel*.

4   *Winter Trees*

Winter Trees, the fourth collection of Sylvia Plath's work, was published in 1971. It is divided into two sections, the first section containing eighteen short poems and the second section containing 'Three Women', a long, dramatic poem written for the BBC. The two sections represent slightly different stages in Sylvia Plath's work; the majority of the poems in the first section were written in the last nine months of her life whereas 'Three Women' was completed rather earlier as it was pre-recorded by the BBC on 2 August 1962 for transmission on 13 September 1962. It thus seems sensible to deal with the book as representative of two stages and to look at these stages in chronological order.

The raw material of Sylvia Plath's work can be found in the events of her own life very often, but 'Three Women' is an indication of her ability to write about situations which have only the smallest coincidence to these events. It could be argued that in a very general way she used her experience of pregnancy and motherhood in the creation of the Wife, and that her own miscarriage gave her an insight into the Secretary's situation. Similarly the home of the Wife is fairly clearly a description of the poet's own Devon home and the University which the Girl attends is probably influenced by Sylvia Plath's memories of her two years at Cambridge. However, beyond this very superficial level of correspondence 'Three Women' is less overtly autobiographical than either *The Bell Jar* or much of the poetry.

'Three Women', which was specially commissioned by the BBC Third Programme, as it then was, is a piece of work in which the author moved away from her autobiographical stance to embody some dominant themes in three different aspects of and attitudes towards one situation. The technique of poems such as 'Lady Lazarus' and 'Daddy' which quite deliberately reveal that the mask of the persona only cursorily disguises the self of the poet

51

moderates in 'Three Women' into a transference of the internal conflicts into external dramatic terms—a technique which is also apparent in poems such as 'Surgeon at 2 a.m.', 'Paralytic' and 'Insomniac'. The poet adopts a more conventional transmutation of her artistic material into the created forms of her art, than in the intricate blend of creation and autobiography which the reader is to believe he receives from the *Ariel* poems, where Sylvia Plath's intention, at least in some degree, was avowedly correspondent to Lowell's aim in *Life Studies*. Lowell himself has said of *Life Studies*:[1]

> They're not always factually true. There's a good deal of tinkering with fact. You leave out a lot, and emphasise this and not that. Your actual experience is a complete flux. I've invented facts and changed things, and the whole balance of the poem was something invented. So there's a lot of artistry, I hope, in the poems. Yet there's this thing: if a poem is autobiographical—and this is true of any kind of autobiographical writing and of historical writing—you want the reader to say, this is true. In something like Macaulay's *History of England* you think you're really getting William 111. That's as good as a good plot in a novel. And so there was always that standard of truth which you wouldn't ordinarily have in poetry —the reader was to believe he was getting the real Robert Lowell.

As 'Three Women' resists any but the most superficial biographical explication and must be discussed in internal terms it provides a useful approach to the work of a poet, who, in most of her works, used autobiography as a structural device, thus rendering objective discussion doubly difficult.

The work describes the experience of three women who are all pregnant. Deliberate alienation seems to be intended in the choice of labels rather than names for the characters; however the refusal to particularise also extends the area of reference of the poem; the three experiences become typical rather than individual. The

1. 'Interview with Robert Lowell', *Paris Review*, spring 1961, p. 70.

characters are realised through their reactions to circumstances, and the external events are resolved in all three cases. The Wife moves from pregnancy through labour to motherhood; the Girl renounces the illegitimate daughter she has borne to return to her university life, while the Secretary's miscarriage results in a retreat into the routine of daily living as a compensation for the lack of maternal fulfilment. The Wife's experience is pivotal; that of the Girl and the Secretary being implicitly compared and contrasted with it, and in this sense the work is dramatic in the juxtaposition and cross-cutting from one woman to another. However the three characters do not communicate directly with each other; the experience of each is developed through an internal, subjective monologue and functions as a self-contained unit, having reference to narrated events beyond the immediate reference of the poem.

Sylvia Plath explores in 'Three Women' the subject of creativity as it is revealed in three separate situations and it is on the Wife's central experience that she dwells in greatest detail. The introspective state of mind which accompanies her pregnancy introduces a vision of herself as a completely self-contained and peaceful microcosm:

> I am slow as the world. I am very patient,
> Turning through my time, the suns and stars
> Regarding me with attention.

The state of being pregnant has for the Wife an ordered inevitability of outcome which is a welcome relief from the necessity of disciplining thought and action: 'I do not have to think, or even rehearse./What happens in me will happen without attention.' The personality has retreated into itself, concentrating on the coming birth and rejecting any other considerations as irrelevant, but the feeing of self-sufficiency of pregnancy gradually develops into one of isolation. During the labour the metamorphic nature of the experience is again emphasised: the mother must endure something akin to physical death to give birth to the child which will be a further proof of her identity; the world image of the first verse is now repeated but its slow and rhythmic turning has been replaced by a convulsive fragmentation:

> A power is growing on me, an old tenacity.
> I am breaking apart like the world. There is this
>   blackness,
> This ram of blackness. I fold my hands on a mountain.
> The air is thick. It is thick with this working.
> I am used. I am drummed into use.
> My eyes are squeezed by this blackness.
> I see nothing.

The actual birth of the child immediately arouses feelings of protectiveness and tenderness in the mother, who acknowledges the miraculous metamorphosis of birth by questioning the value of her earlier life. However a transition is affected between the mother's protectiveness towards the child and her wish that he will be some solace to her; the microcosmic experience of pregnancy, which engendered complete self-confidence, has been replaced by a sense of the alienated individual isolated in a hostile universe which runs through much of Sylvia Plath's work and which we have come to see as being part of the modern predicament. The suggestion is that the mother cannot protect the child fully because of her own fears and inadequacies and also that the presence of the child does not provide a sufficiently strong charm against the prevailing despair and menace of the mother's world:

> How long can I be a wall, keeping the wind off?
> How long can I be
> Gentling the sun with the shade of my hand,
> Intercepting the blue bolts of a cold moon?
> The voices of loneliness, the voices of sorrow
> Lap at my back ineluctably.
> How shall it soften them, this little lullaby?

The sense of isolation is eventually replaced by reassurance as the mother makes a conscious effort to relinquish fears and immerse herself in the normality of her son; these earlier fears are now realised in a reference to deformed children who provide a terrible, grotesque parody of the perfection of her son:

> I do not believe in those terrible children
> Who injure my sleep with their white eyes, their
>   fingerless hands.
> They are not mine. They do not belong to me.

If this reference on the symbolical level is to spiritual fears, on the actual level it may well have been prompted by the thalidomide tragedy of the early sixties. The imagery of 'Thalidomide', which dates from about the same time, is very similar and suggests that the poet, as one might expect, was very disturbed by the reports of deformity. They were a further reflection of one of her recurrent fears.

The Secretary's miscarriage is an indication for her of her failure which is both physical and spiritual. She associates her infertility with an inability to live naturally, without an over-attentive awareness of the consequences of her actions. Her history of miscarriages becomes evidence of the predatory savagery of an earth which exacts frequent sacrifices, as a placation for the misdeeds of men, and which will eventually 'eat them in the end' as their bodies return to the earth after death. The only possible escape from this continuous cycle of infertility and agony is into the peripheral area of daily living, for the progression of hope and failure can only be broken by a rejection of the whole struggle, and a withdrawal into a more secure if rather arid state:

> I shall be a heroine of the peripheral.
> I shall not be accused by isolate buttons,
> Holes in the heels of socks, the white mute faces
> Of unanswered letters, coffined in a letter case.

The Secretary's experience in hospital has been one of immersion in pain and loss of identity. Leaving hospital is accompanied by a painful assumption of identity symbolised in the reparation of external normality. She dons a 'face' to meet the world. Although she comforts herself with the possibility of success next time her physical neatness is a misleading mask beneath which bitterness still triumphs as she tastes: 'The incalculable malice of the everyday'. This is finally replaced by a sad acceptance of the inevitability of her position underlain by a slight suggestion of renewed hope:

> The city waits and aches. The little grasses
> Crack through stone, and they are green with life.

The Secretary's desire that life should be consequential, that specific acts should be followed by expected results is ironically matched with the Girl's revulsion from the consequential progression of living, of which her pregnancy is seen as a hateful result of 'Every little word hooked to every little word, and act to act'. The Wife's calm expectancy: 'I am ready' finds an echo in the Girl's desperate wish to undo the consequences of her act: 'I wasn't ready'. Unable to deny or break loose from the consequential progression of events the Girl continues with the pregnancy, reflecting when it is too late: 'I should have murdered this, that murders me'. The birth of her daughter replaces the old bitterness at the inescapable physical event by a new grief as she consciously chooses to relinquish the child. She is at last able to deny the consequence but only with considerable pain to herself:

> I am so vulnerable suddenly.
> I am a wound walking out of hospital.
> I am a wound that they are letting go.
> I leave my health behind. I leave someone
> Who would adhere to me: I undo her fingers like
>   bandages: I go.

She returns to her university life but finds herself unable to cast off the sense of loss which she sees reflected in her natural surroundings.

There is little in Sylvia Plath's work which is overtly religious in any conventional sense although Lois Ames has indicated that she had a religious family background,[2] but underlying 'Three Women' is a fairly substantial structure of Christian reference. The first of these references occurs in the Secretary's opening

2. 'Notes Toward a Biography', Lois Ames in *The Art of Sylvia Plath*, p. 157.

speech: she sees the flatness of the non-pregnant body as a source of various types of destruction, physical and spiritual, including: 'The cold angels, the abstractions'. Later she refers to 'the cold angel' in a way that suggests that it may be the angel of death: 'am I a pulse/That wanes and wanes, facing the cold angel?/Is this my lover then? This death, this death?'. 'Magi', now collected in *Crossing the Water*, has a similar reference. A mother addresses her six-month-old child who is unaware of and therefore shielded from the forces of Good and Evil around her cot, described in the following terms: 'The abstracts hover like dull angels . . . They're/ The real thing, all right: the Good, the True.' The child is immersed in the utterly simple physical wants which form the horizons of her world, and is completely impervious to the abstracts, which are real only for her mother:

> For her, the heavy notion of Evil
>
> Attending her cot is less than a belly ache,
> And Love the mother of milk, no theory.

The Girl sees the swans on the river as the natural representation of the events which are bearing down on her, and her reaction is: 'There is a snake in swans', which contains some reference to the temptation of Eve by the serpent and the whole question of original sin—it may also recall the rape of Leda. She is burdened by the consequences of her act specifically because: 'I had no reverence.' The Secretary thinks of her miscarried children as being in a state of holiness in death which is the only possible state of perfection, an idea which occurs constantly in Sylvia Plath's late work, but in this case she extends the reference into specifically Christian terms: the flatness of infertility is associated with the flatness of the male body and the prime example of this can be identified in God, who, through Christ, assumed the body of a man. In her bitterness the Secretary suggests that the flatness of the non-pregnant woman is God-sent and that her own infertility is part of a Divine plan:

> It is these men I mind:
> They are so jealous of anything that is not flat! They
> are jealous gods

That would have the whole world flat because they are.
I see the Father conversing with the Son.
Such flatness cannot but be holy.
'Let us make a heaven,' they say.
'Let us flatten and launder the grossness from these
    souls.'

The Wife waiting for her labour to begin describes herself as a
Mary: 'Dusk hoods me in blue like a Mary', a comparison which
is elaborated towards the end of the poem. Labour itself she
describes as a 'miracle' and the inescapable biblical connotations
of the word, together with her description of herself as a Mary
suggest a Christian reference. The Secretary's experience of loss is
similarly described in terms suggestive of another part of the
Christian story:

I am accused. I dream of massacres.
I am a garden of black and red agonies. I drink them,
Hating myself, hating and fearing. . . .

The metaphor of drinking in association with pain is an echo of
Christ's prayer of 'Take away this cup'. As the mother muses on
her newborn son she sees the innocent inexperience of the child in
terms of the traditional Christian conception of the innocence and
purity of the newly born who are in a state of grace. Again birth is
'miraculous' and the miracle is contained in the potential hope
which each child brings into the world. However the most remarkable and open reference to Christianity appears in the Wife's
expression of her wishes for the child's future, which pick up her
earlier references to herself as a Mary, as well as the slight identification of her child with the infant Christ contained in the reference to him as 'still swaddled in white bands'; she states:

I do not will him to be exceptional.
It is the exception that interests the devil.
It is the exception that climbs the sorrowful hill
Or sits in the desert and hurts his mother's heart.

The sorrowful hill is clearly Calvary and the desert recalls Christ's
temptation in the wilderness.

It does not seem to be part of the poet's intention that any Christian or philosophical conclusion shall be stated through the accumulation of these references; there is no discussion or statement as such, rather the Christian references are employed for their symbolic value. Christ's Passion and Sacrifice are symbols for the Secretary of suffering and for the Wife of the pain she wishes to avert, rather than references worked into a predominantly Christian view of life, to which the experiences of the characters are subordinated. The conclusions which are reached are indicated less through any rational statement than through the imagistic structure of the poem which establishes a basic opposition between the forces of fertility and those of infertility. Contrast forms the structural basis of much of Sylvia Plath's work and the opposition established in 'Three Women' is another manifestation of the comparison between light and dark, good and evil, life and death which was the focus of her imagination. Certain images become typically associated with fertility in 'Three Women', chief among which is the group concerned with trees, flowers and grasses. The greater number of these occur in the stanzas spoken by the Wife, who is able to achieve and happily accept fertility, in contrast to the Secretary's inability to carry a child to term, and the Girl's desire to renounce her fertility.

At the beginning of the poem the Wife states: 'Leaves and petals attend me' and this reference is elaborated when her sense of momentousness before labour is concentrated in a very similar image:

> I am calm. I am calm. It is the calm before something
> awful:
> The yellow minute before the wind walks, when the
> leaves
> Turn up their hands, their pallors. . . .

She identifies her heavy body with a swollen seed about to burst into flower, but because the process of flowering or birth necessarily involves the decay and death of the old self an image of natural death is used: 'The trees wither in the street. The rain is corrosive.' A particularly Plathian effect is achieved in the description of the placenta: 'red lotus opens in its bowl of blood', one of the more extreme of the many fascinated references to blood and bleeding which stud the later poetry. Nature imagery describes the fragility and sweetness of the newborn child: 'His lids are like the lilac-flowers/And soft as a moth, his breath' for the relationship of reliant child and mother is that of a plant towards the sun: 'He is turning to me like a little, blind, bright plant.' A detailing of natural surroundings in ecstatic terms accompanies the return of assurance after fear at the end of the poem, and the plant imagery finds expression in the use of 'flowers' as a verb: 'Dawn flowers in the great elm outside the house.'

Occasionally images of the plant group are included in the stanzas spoken by the Secretary but always, with one important exception, as images of decay, withering, pain. As her miscarriage begins she reflects: 'I saw a death in the bare trees', and at the height of her agony cries out: 'I am a garden of black and red agonies.' As she leaves the hospital, thinking with bitterness of her own infertility she sees it reflected in the bare winter twigs: 'These little black twigs do not think to bud'; but recovering physically and emotionally she begins to hope again, and with the coming of spring grass forces its way through the obdurate and barren stones of the city: 'The city waits and aches. The little grasses/crack through stone, and they are green with life.'

The very few tree, flower, grass images embodied in the Girl's stanzas are orientated towards notions of loneliness and vulnerability. The moment of knowledge of pregnancy is sharpened by an awareness of the hostility of her surroundings: 'The willows were chilling'; but after the birth the flowers in her room become a symbol of vulnerability with a dual reference to her own emotional and the child's physical state:

> The flowers in this room are red and tropical.
> They have lived behind glass all their lives, they have been cared for tenderly.
> Now they face a winter of white sheets, white faces.

A rather similar imagistic complex occurs in 'Tuplis', where the red flowers are also compared to the white stillness of the hospital ward, although there they provide an unwelcome note of vitality which dominates and eventually disrupts the whiteness of negation, pulling the patient unwillingly back to health; here it is clear that they themselves will be swallowed up in the whiteness. After the Girl returns to University although she sees around her the beauty of a hot summer's day her own subjective state remains one of unrelieved loneliness: 'I am solitary as grass.'

Imagery drawn from the plant world suggests fertility, but infertility is related to a world of torture and pain where technical knowledge is harnessed to the destructive will. The flatness of her miscarriage becomes for the Secretary a further indication of the malice and evil of a world in which man has used his intellect to devise means of torture and death, 'That flat, flat, flatness from which ideas, destructions,/Bulldozers, guillotines, white chambers of shrieks proceed'. Sylvia Plath identifies ideas with destruction, and there is a sense running through 'Three Women' that one should not think too much—the Wife exults in her pregnancy because it will proceed without the necessity for willed action on her part, and the Secretary claims that she has 'tried not to think too hard'. The work forcefully establishes a well-pointed contrast between the natural world, which proceeds in an ordered cycle of living and dying, and the man-made world, which attempts to control this cycle by human means.

The Secretary's reference to a white chamber is echoed as the Girl waits for labour to begin: 'I have seen the white clean chamber with its instruments./It is a place of shrieks. It is not happy.' The creation of the Girl modulates the basic contrast between fertility and sterility suggested by the Wife and the Secretary. Because she acknowledges her fertility only unwillingly she experiences both the maternal tenderness of the Wife and the pain and grief of the Secretary; Sylvia Plath is careful not to formulate too rigidly schematic an opposition, but she does suggest that the Girl's eventual unhappiness stems from her refusal to accept her fertility.

The association of hospitals, pain and illness with torture is not an uncommon one, but it is a fairly insistent motif in the work of Sylvia Plath and can be ultimately related to her concern with the concentration camps. In *The Bell Jar* she again compares the labour table to a torture table:

> It looked like some awful torture table, with these
> metal stirrups sticking up in mid-air at one end and all
> sorts of instruments and wires and tubes I couldn't
> make out properly at the other.

This comparison forms part of a larger imagistic motif of the novel; the reference to torture is a reminder of an image which occurs earlier in the book:

> and the glittering white torture-chamber tiles under my
> feet and over my head and on all four sides closed in
> and squeezed me to pieces.

It also relates forward to a later incident when Dr Nolan takes Esther through the basement of the hospital to the E.C.T. room (it is no coincidence that they return through the autumn leaves):

> The walls were bright, white lavatory tile with bald
> bulbs set at intervals in the black ceiling.

Sylvia Plath stated that hers was an art in which image and symbol are often related to preoccupations beyond the specific area of the poem:[3]

> The issues of our time which preoccupy me at the
> moment are the incalculable genetic effects of fall-out
> and a documentary article on the terrifying, mad,
> omnipotent marriage of big business and the military
> in America—'Juggernaut, The Warfare State', by Fred
> J. Cook in a recent *Nation*. Does this influence the kind
> of poetry that I write? Yes, but in a sidelong fashion. I
> am not gifted with the tongue of Jeremiah, though I
> may be sleepless enough before my vision of the
> Apocalypse. My poems do not turn out to be about
> Hiroshima, but about a child forming itself finger by
> finger in the dark. They are not about the terrors of
> mass extinction, but about the bleakness of the moon
> over a yew tree in a neighbouring graveyard. Not

3. 'Context', London Magazine, 2 (n.s.), 1962, pp. 45–6.

about the testaments of tortured Algerians but about
the night thoughts of a tired surgeon.

If we turn to a poem such as 'Lady Lazarus', which is more
explicitly concerned with the political issues of recent history, we
begin to appreciate the wider significances which the references to
torture had for her. Images of torture occur at moments of stress in
both *The Bell Jar* and 'Three Women'; in 'Lady Lazarus' the
most disturbing events of her own life, her suicide attempts, are
directly related to the most disturbing events of the century—the
experiences of those interned in the concentration camps. In
'Three Women', as in the later work, public and private are fused
together, although in 'Three Women' the dramatic situation still
dominates the personal concerns.

'Three Women' implicitly suggests that the fertility of the
woman is opposed to the 'flatness' of the man and it is from
flatness that 'ideas, destructions,/Bulldozers, guillotines, white
chambers of shrieks proceed'. The imagery of the poem establishes
the opposition; pregnancy, which symbolises spiritual and mental
as well as physical creativity, is described in a progression of images
drawn from the vegetation cycle, whereas infertility, which con-
versely represents spiritual aridity, is imagistically associated with
the human world in all its more terrible aspects.

The eighteen poems collected in the first half of *Winter Trees*
were all written in the last nine months of Sylvia Plath's life and
are thus contemporary to the *Ariel* poems. In his brief introductory note to *Winter Trees* Ted Hughes describes the poems in
Ariel, also published posthumously, as being 'more or less arbi-
trarily chosen' and certainly the best poems in *Winter Trees*, 'The
Rabbit Catcher', 'Mary's Song', 'Child', are as good as anything
in *Ariel*, but the quality of the achievement is uneven; *Winter
Trees* is not so accomplished a collection as *Ariel*. The last poems
which were offered for publication by the poet herself came from
the period now represented by *Crossing the Water*, consequently we
do not know if she would have rejected any of the late poems. We
do know that she ruthlessly revised and destroyed many of her
earlier poems. At least four of the poems in *Winter Trees*, 'Lyonnesse', 'Purdah', 'The Rabbit Catcher' and 'Stopped Dead', had
been written by the end of October 1962 as these four were

among the poems which Sylvia Plath read for the British Council recording, although 'Lyonnesse' was then entitled 'Amnesiac'. A revised version of 'Stopped Dead' was published in *London Magazine* in January 1963 and there are slight revisions in the versions of 'Purdah' and 'Amnesiac' included in *Winter Trees*. It seems clear that in the period of great creativity which was ended by her tragic death Sylvia Plath was constantly reworking her material, reshaping and revising poems, sometimes cutting them brutally. The internal evidence of the poems also suggests some reworking —'By Candlelight', for instance, includes lines which were originally part of 'Nick and the Candlestick'. What was one poem at the end of October 1962 became two poems on the same subject but with a different mood by early February 1963.

One of the most noticeable aspects of *Winter Trees* is the recurrence of certain subjects and images, many of them also figure in *Ariel*. The poems can be divided into two groups—those which are recognisably domestic and personal and those with a dramatic focus—although in the latter group also the concern is ultimately a personal one. To describe Sylvia Plath's subject as 'domestic' is not to diminish it in any way, for, as in *Ariel*, these poems move from a limited private world to a limitless public one. The best example of this width of reference undoubtedly appears in 'Mary's Song', which had already and deservedly been widely anthologised before its inclusion in this volume. Mary, Christ, God are frequently referred to in *Winter Trees*, although as has already been noted in relation to 'Three Women' Sylvia Plath's intention was never doctrinal; she uses Christianity as one element in the drama of her own poetic world, but gives equal value to the mythological and classical figures who still move through this world although less dominantly now than in *The Colossus*. 'Mary's Song' is strangely named for the poem emerges as a lamentation rather than a celebration. It begins calmly, domestically, with the Sunday joint cooking in the oven—three of the most anguished poems, 'Lesbos', 'Mary's Song' and 'A Birthday Present', begin in the unremarkable and unlikely setting of a kitchen. But the first line of the poem immediately conducts us into a world of religious persecution and sacrifice where heretics are burnt at the stake and the smoke from the gas ovens of the twentieth century floats over Europe. For Mary the suffering is personal for the repeated 'holocaust' of history is contained in her heart as she contemplates the baby whose sacrifice will not prevent suffering, indeed it will engender a new form of persecution. The poem is economical and disciplined and the mood less hysterical than in some of the later poems. It even has its own strange beauty, the smoke clouds of the ovens hanging over Germany and Poland have the melancholy beauty of utter desolation: 'Grey birds obsess my heart,/Mouth-ash, ash of eye.' 'Mary's Song' belongs to the group of political poems collected in *Ariel*—'Daddy', 'Lady Lazarus', 'Fever 103°' and it appears with them in the American edition of *Ariel*.

Increasingly the poems of these last nine months become a cry of sheer outrage, sometimes expressed with the disciplined economy of 'Mary's Song', sometimes more savagely forced from her as in 'Gigolo'. In 'The Courage of Shutting Up' Sylvia Plath systematically converts everything which disturbed her in the external world into a metaphor to illustrate her personal experience. The poem encapsulates many of the recurrent themes— tattooing, hospitals, armaments, mirrors, politics—they all appear frequently in the late poetry and in the prose. In 'The Courage of Shutting Up' the poet feels that the savage, unremitting violence of existence may be faced with true courage in silence rather than protest. The brain revolves mechanically always charting suffering, it encounters no beauty or relief and fights to disrupt the apparent calm of the closed lips. The tongue could destroy complacency by giving utterance to the mind's grotesque perceptions but it too is suppressed; it is only in the eyes that one might see the inner torture reflected, but even the eyes show only the blank deadness of a fight which is nearly over:

> They may be white and shy, they are no stool pigeons,
> Their death rays folded like flags
> Of a country no longer heard of,
> An obstinate independency
> Insolvent among the mountains.

The courage lies in living with the knowledge of outrage and not seeking the relief of utterance. The poem is, in many ways, typical of the very personal voice which emerges from Sylvia Plath's late work. The use of question marks, exclamation marks, dashes adds to the appearance of easy fluency—Ted Hughes has described his wife's poetry as being written in 'direct, and even plain speech'.[4] The simple statements, the voice of the poet directly addressing the reader also contribute to this effect. However the stylistic simplicity is counterpointed by an agility and speed of association and reference which is also characteristic of the late work. The mind which produced poetry of this order was an intensely intelligent one striving to cope with and contain its particular vision of the truth.

Each poem expresses the dilemmas of her vision and the tensions and opposites are stated with growing and painful precision. Such a poem is 'The Rabbit Catcher'. The poem starts uncompromisingly: 'It was a place of force'—and it soon becomes apparent that the force is both external and self-engendered, the wind whips away her voice, the sea blinds her with its reflections but she herself is the agent of this violence: 'The wind gagging my mouth with my own blown hair.' The persona's reactions to her surroundings are so raw and immediate that all extremes of feeling are merged into one complex sensation which is both painful and beautiful, and her vision of the gorse bushes becomes a torture of the self in its intensity:

> I tasted the malignity of the gorse,
> Its black spikes,
> The extreme unction of its yellow candle-flowers.
> They had an efficiency, a great beauty,
> And were extravagant, like torture.

The wild tension of wind, sea, gorse forces her inevitably on into a still centre of suffering; she identifies herself with the rabbit who is almost mesmerically lured by the intent concentration of the waiting rabbit-catcher: 'There was only one place to get to.' The sense of unwilling but inevitable progression towards a fixed doom recurs frequently in the late work and is allied to the even more stultifying feeling of complete helplessness expressed in 'The Moon and the Yew Tree': 'I simply cannot see where there is to get to.' The inner world is being sharply defined and it affords no

4. Hughes, 'Notes on the Chronological Order of Sylvia Plath's Poems', *op. cit.*, p. 195.

escape: 'The sack of black! It is everywhere, tight, tight!' The poems reveal a constant tension, expressed in 'Stopped Dead' as being 'hung out over the dead drop' and there is no one to pull her back from the abyss for the question of 'Mystic': 'Is there no great love, only tenderness?' is tacitly answered by a negative.

The dilemma of 'Mystic', which Robert Lowell has described as one of her finest poems, is that of harmonising ecstasy and normality, for the insights of the mystic bring him only pain. The vision of God is one of enormity which leaves no possibility of human fulfilment: 'Once one has seen God, what is the remedy?' Various reactions to normality are examined but rejected and the greatest pain strikes with the reluctant return to the new day with its muted beauty:

> The chimneys of the city breathe, the window sweats,
> The children leap in their cots.
> The sun blooms, it is a geranium.
>
> The heart has not stopped.

Three of the poems in *Winter Trees*, 'Child', 'By Candlelight' and 'For a Fatherless Son' are about the poet's children. They form a group with 'Morning Song', 'The Night Dances', 'Nick and the Candlestick', 'You're' and 'Balloons'. These poems are all expressions of tenderness and protectiveness for the child combined with personal feelings of despair and loneliness. The children represent a world of happiness and effortless peace which is far removed from the dark cruelty of the mother's universe. Frequently she sees them as untainted by her own complexities and in 'Child' feels that the natural clarity of the child is opposed to the mother's dark solitariness:

> Pool in which images
> Should be grand and classical
>
> Not this troublous
> Wringing of hands, this dark
> Ceiling without a star.

She appreciates and envies the child's world because it is capable

67

of indefinite expansion whereas the mother's world is narrowing in to a state of self-enclosure. 'By Candlelight' is a companion poem to 'Nick and the Candlestick' and was probably written in the last three months of the poet's life as it contains lines included in 'Nick and the Candlestick' at the end of October. 'By Candlelight' reminds the reader of Sylvia Plath's lyrical powers for when she allows herself to be purely descriptive as in the opening lines of this poem, she has the ability to evoke atmosphere both visually and in sound:

> This is winter, this is night, small love—
> A sort of black horsehair,
> A rough, dumb country stuff
> Steeled with the sheen
> Of what green stars can make it to our gate.

The picture of mother and child looking out at the dark night quickly and typically becomes a metaphor for the relationship between the mother's unwavering sense of her child's reality and her perception of her own nightmare world with its shifting realities. As she lights the candle, thus revealing the baby, she accepts with delighted wonder that 'one match-scratch makes you real', but as the candle flame burns up brightly it becomes for her an all too transient symbol of a light which must give way to the more powerful and implacable suffocation of the dark night: 'The sack of black! It is everywhere, tight, tight!' It is in this series of poems inspired by her maternal feelings that Sylvia Plath reveals the cruel opposites of her world in their starkest opposition, but they are not black poems because the darkness of the mother's world is subordinated to the light of the child's. The child is loved because of the unselfconscious demands he makes on his mother, but also because, unlike an adult, he sees nothing of her growing depression, of 'the godawful hush' at the core of her existence.

Few of Sylvia Plath's early poems were overtly personal but this later work is almost always centred in personal experience. However the world of inanimate objects also plays an important part in *Winter Trees*; either as part of a surrealist nightmare as in 'The Other':

> Open your handbag. What is that bad smell?
> It is your knitting, busily
>
> Hooking itself to itself,
> It is your sticky candies.

Or, also in 'The Other', as an index of the growing isolation of the persona: 'Cold glass, how you insert yourself/Between myself and myself;' the world is recognisably that of the bell jar with its static vapour. More positively inanimate objects have a sureness and solid identity compared to the flux of human knowledge. In the title poem the poet obliquely compares the trees beyond her window, just visible in the early morning light, to women and finds that the trees have a comforting stability which women lack:

> Knowing neither abortions nor bitchery,
> Truer than women,
> They seed so effortlessly!

This poem again emphasises the structural difference between *The Colossus* and the later work. Like 'Sheep in Fog' and 'The Moon and the Yew Tree' it begins with an acute visual description of the external world but moves rapidly into the inner landscape. In *The Colossus* the mind usually stayed in the outer world, analysing and commenting on it; in *Winter Trees* and *Ariel* we are always returned to the inner, icy world of pain and alienation. Significantly enough *The Colossus* poems are mostly daytime poems; Sylvia Plath herself pointed out that most of her later poems were written in the very early morning, a time of introversion and stillness.[5]

5. 'Sylvia Plath', A. Alvarez, The Art of Sylvia Plath, p. 59.

5   *Ariel*

Ariel, the posthumous volume of Sylvia Plath's poetry published in 1965 by Faber and Faber is not the collection of several years' writing as was the first book *The Colossus*. The majority of the poems in *Ariel* were written between the end of September 1962 and the date of her death on 11 February 1963. 'You're', the earliest poem in the book, belongs to early 1960;[1] many of the poems now collected in *Crossing the Water* were written between 'You're' and 'Tulips', which was written in March 1961[2] and recalls the time Sylvia Plath spent in hospital recovering from her appendectomy. 'Morning Song', a poem written for her daughter, Frieda, dates from a short time afterwards, and 'Little Fugue', inspired by Beethoven's 'Grosse Fugue', was written in the autumn of 1961. 'Elm', a poem describing an elm tree outside the Devon house, belongs to March 1962 and was followed by 'The Moon and the Yew Tree', written at the suggestion of Ted Hughes who was impressed by the picture of a full moon over the yew tree in the neighbouring graveyard. 'The Rival' was written in the late spring or early summer of 1962 and 'Berck-Plage' came shortly afterwards; it records a holiday spent by the Hughes in France in 1961 and also refers to the death of a neighbour in June 1962. October and November of 1962 inaugurated a period of great creative fertility for Sylvia Plath who wrote, according to Ted Hughes, everything else in *Ariel* up to the end of the bee sequence. 'Munich Mannequins' and 'Totem', companion poems written during two days, belong to mid-January 1963 as does 'Paralytic' also. 'Balloons', 'Contusion', 'Kindness', 'Edge' and Words' were written in the last weeks of the poet's life.

The world of *Ariel* is bleak, despairing, grotesque; maimed

1. Hughes, *op. cit.*, p. 192.
2. *Ibid.*, p. 193. See this article for all the chronological references in this chapter.

human beings call hopelessly to each other and are ignored. In such a world 'Love is a shadow', and marriage is a final, desperate attempt to achieve solace and communication, but even marriage is bitterly rejected by the poet as an artificiality which brings only pain: 'A ring of gold with the sun in it?/Lies. Lies and a grief.' Some relief can be found in the innocence and unselfconscious beauty of children, but the experience is searing, dragging the feelings back from the black well of depression:

> So your gestures flake off—
>
> Warm and human, then their pink light
> Bleeding and peeling
>
> Through the black amnesias of heaven.

The setting is a domestic one; there are references to children, to cooking, to beekeeping, to balloons which have decorated a Christmas room, but it is a domesticity wrenched from its usual context of familiarity and comfortably unassuming security. A savage yearning for a violent suicide dominates the mind of the woman whose hands regularly, surely, make pastry, who moves round the kitchen efficiently preparing food to sustain a life which she finds unbearable. A mother anxiously awake in the early morning, attentive to her daughter's least cry, is also aware of the loneliness of self which encloses each individual in a stony separateness:

> Our voices echo, magnifying your arrival. New statue.
> In a drafty museum, your nakedness
> Shadows our safety. We stand round blankly as walls.

'Tulips', one of the longer poems, is in many ways typical, although formally it differs from the majority of the poems. It is written in seven line verses, whereas most of the poems have verses of either five or three lines. The line is also longer than usual, 'Berck-Plage', 'The Moon and the Yew Tree', 'A Birthday Present' and 'The Bee Meeting' are the only other poems with lines of a comparable length. The tone of the poem has neither the hysterical gaiety of 'The Applicant' and 'Cut', nor the anguish of 'Elm' or 'Little Fugue'; it is informed by a more reflective

71

melancholy as the persona broods on the state of mind induced by her situation as a patient in hospital. The world of the hospital ward is a welcome one of snowy whiteness and silence, in which the woman grasps eagerly at the ability to relax completely because nothing is required of her. She has moved beyond normal activity, and relishes the opportunity to relinquish all responsibility, to become a 'body' with no personal identity:

> I have given my name and my day-clothes up to the
>   nurses
> And my history to the anaesthetist and my body to
>   surgeons.

The renunciation of individuality also includes the reduction of others to a depersonalised level, so that they make no claims on her and she is aware of making none on them; consequently she sees the nurses hurrying about the ward as being as alike as a flock of gulls flying inland. She sees herself as an inanimate object, a pebble. The apprehension of self as a concrete, inanimate object, a thing, is one which occurs frequently in *Ariel*; in 'Morning Song' the object is a statue, in 'Getting There' a letter in a slot, in 'The Bee Meeting' 'milkweed silk'. The poems move with increasing certainty towards a renunciation of personality, an attempt to escape conflicts and fears by becoming incapable of them. The desire to reduce awareness even includes the necessity to dissociate self from the family relationships which drag the patient back from the white oblivion of the numbness she cultivates. Banishing family ties, material possessions and 'loving associations' brings fear as well as peace, but this is compensated for by the new freedom which is associated with religion: the state of mind achieved recalls the purity of a nun; death is usually pure in *Ariel* because it brings escape from conflict; it symbolises a rebirth, and all the pain and torture of living described in 'Getting There' ends in the purity of death:

> And I, stepping from this skin
> Of old bandages, boredoms, old faces
>
> Step to you from the black car of Lethe,
> Pure as a baby.

Similarly at the end of 'A Birthday Present' the thought of a particularly violent death is again associated with purity and birth because it brings peace:

> And the knife not carve, but enter
>
> Pure and clean as the cry of a baby,
> And the universe slide from my side.

The tulips erupt into the whiteness of the microcosm the patient has created as a painful reminder of the health which she consciously strives to reject. The world of *Ariel* is a black and white one into which red, which represents blood, the heart and living, is always an intrusion. The tulips hurt because they require the emotional response which will rouse her from the numbness of complete mental and physical inactivity; she feels that the flowers have eyes which watch her and increase her sense of her own unreality: 'And I see myself, flat, ridiculous, a cut-paper shadow/ Between the eye of the sun and the eye of the tulips.' This sense of unreality, of substancelessness, is not similar to the feeling of immersion in self which she has cultivated, it is a sense of inadequacy and alienation also described in 'Cut': 'I have taken a pill to kill/The thin/Papery feeling.' Eventually the tulips force her attention into focus and she merges from the world of whiteness and silence to a not unpleasurable anticipation:

> And I am aware of my heart: it opens and closes
> Its bowl of red blooms out of sheer love of me.
> The water I taste is warm and salt, like the sea,
> And comes from a country far away as health.

Although 'Tulips' is written in the present tense it has less of the immediacy of some of the later poems in *Ariel* because the element of control exhibited in the meditative focus and the fashioning of thought and feeling into logically connected statements operates as a distancing device. 'The Moon and the Yew Tree', one of the finest poems in *Ariel*, also exhibits this taut control of mood. The external details of the full moon shining over the yew tree in a neighbouring graveyard are internalised and allowed to approximate to states of mind; the outer bleakness and loneliness correspond to an inner loneliness, in which the mind becomes a graveyard because the persona has reached a state of ultimate despair from which she can see no escape, no progression: 'I simply cannot see where there is to get to.' The poem emphasises that the woman feels at home in such an environment; a row of headstones actually separates the graveyard from her house and the feeling of depression and spiritual death which the graveyard represents for her is equally close. Above the graveyard shines a moon which provides no relief; it symbolises a world of absolute despair in itself which is accepted by the persona:

> The moon is no door. It is a face in its own right,
> White as a knuckle and terribly upset.
> It drags the sea after it like a dark crime; it is quiet
> With the O-gape of complete despair. I live here.

In such a world of death and darkness the church bells 'startle the sky' as they affirm that resurrection has followed death, and that the world of the graveyard and the moon need not be a final one. Although the woman would like to accept the promises of religion the world of the moon subjects her and she is forced to reject the tenderness she strives for: 'The moon is my mother. She is not sweet like Mary.' However although the interior of the church represents a world of hope and love opposed to the bleakness of the graveyard, it is itself presented with some ambivalence. 'Cold' and 'stiff', words usually associated with death, suggest that the world of the church is not completely divorced from that of the grave-yard. Interpretation of the degree of hopelessness in the last verse depends partly on an evaluation of the word 'blue'. In the first verse the poet states that the light of the mind is blue, the trees black; if the trees, the things which grow in the mind, are thoughts, then the 'light' may be the imagination, in which case Sylvia Plath's use of the colour corresponds to Wallace Steven's use of it. In the third verse 'blue' describes the robes of the moon with which the poet has claimed kinship. It thus acquires connotations of the ideas and feelings associated with the moon throughout *Ariel*. In the final verse the word is used twice:

> I have fallen a long way. Clouds are flowering
> Blue and mystical over the face of the stars.

Inside the church, the saints will be all blue,
Floating on their delicate feet over the cold pews,
Their hands and faces stiff with holiness.

This last verse strengthens the suggestion of the first verse that
'blue' is a colour of the mind, and opposes the blueness of clouds
and saints to the starkness of the graveyard where there is only the
bleak contrast of black yew tree and white moon, but the connotations which the colour has acquired in the third verse devalue its
use in this final verse, as does the juxtaposition of it to the word
'cold' which introduces the sense of 'blue with cold'. Lois Ames
quotes a letter from Sylvia Plath which indicates that she did find
the Anglican religion a grimly forbidding one:[3]

> I think our little local church very lovely—it has 8
> bellringers and some fine stained-glass windows, but I
> must say the Anglican religion seems terribly numb and
> cold and grim to me . . . All the awful emphasis on our
> weakness and sinfulness and being able to do nothing
> but through Christ . . . But I do want Frieda to have
> the experience of Sunday School, so I may keep up the
> unsatisfactory practice of going, although I disagree
> with almost everything.

In general terms 'The Moon and the Yew Tree' visualises the
proximity of two worlds, the world of absolute despair symbolised
by the graveyard with its attendant yew tree and moon, and the
world of affirmation and tenderness represented by the church
which, although it has some aura of coldness and stiffness, contains the effigy which 'gentled by candles' has mild eyes. The
poet's world is the first one where identity loses itself in the bald
bleakness; but despite the darkness of both mindscape and landscape the poem has a melancholic lyricism; the icy world is
delineated with a strength which to some extent denies the
apparent despair.

A poem which was written in October 1962 although it was
later revised, 'Nick and the Candlestick', has a first line which
also indicates that Sylvia Plath occasionally used the colour 'blue'

3. Ames, *op. cit.*, p. 170.

as a description of a state of mind: 'I am a miner. The light burns blue.' Primarily the word is descriptive of the candle flame, but the poem develops the technique of 'The Moon and the Yew Tree' by making the descriptions of the outer world into symbols and images for the poet's inner life. A mother sits nursing her baby by candlelight and the effect of the light on the room leads her to imagine that she is a miner in the depths of the earth and the candle becomes a lamp showing her the way forward through caves where, 'Waxy stalactites/Drip and thicken'. The picture of the stalactites can be related to the wax dripping down the sides of the candle for there are three levels in this poem: that of the actual scene where mother and child sit in a candlelit room, that of the imagined miner in the underground caves and that of the state of mind for which the first part of the poem becomes an image. The subterranean world is an unpleasant one of coldness, blackness, dampness, where various forces and entities attack the miner in an attempt to devour or reduce him. The mood here is bleak but as the candlelight strengthens the mother's thoughts turn to the child whose sleep she watches over and who represents another world of clearness, warmth and beauty which forms a direct contrast to the underground violence her mind has rejected. The child is tainted by no hereditary imperfection, even though he wakes to a world which contains his mother's pain, he does not share it. Although the mother accepts that she cannot herself escape the horrors of her existence—a double threat which is seen in the extinction of the stars and the man-made extinction of the atom-bomb—the child has a solidity of being, a promise of security, which redeem the blackness of the first half of the poem. The final reference has clear religious overtones: 'You are the the baby in the barn' and is contrasted with the 'piranha/ Religion' of the first half; similarly the cave in which the miner wanders is matched in the second half, but it is now a place of beauty and warmth, created by the mother out of love for her child:

> Love, love,
> I have hung our cave with roses,
> With soft rugs—
>
> The last of Victoriana.

Sylvia Plath develops the poem through associations and images; the logic is inner and arbitrary and she accomplishes the progression of the poem from fear and depression to qualified optimism and happiness through the movement from the imagery of the first half to the direct statements of the second half. The moment of transition between the two parts is achieved when the candle flame burns more brightly, drawing the mother from her brooding, introverted fears into a consideration of the promise of her son. The technique of the first half of the poem is similar to that of 'Night Dances', another poem written at about this time and also occasioned by her son, Nicholas. The lines of the first half of 'Nick and the Candlestick' are short and jerky; they echo the path of the mind as it moves disjointedly from one thought to another. The poet's imagination lays itself open to an impression, an image, which is then developed freely. As the poem moves from the fantastic grotesquerie of the first part to the stronger affirmation of the second, the lines become smoother, the thought units longer.

The subject of 'Nick and the Candlestick' is domestic and throughout *Ariel* the domestic and simple incidents of daily living are effortlessly translated into images of the terrible inner experiences of the poet; landscape reflects mindscape. The delicacy and skill with which Sylvia Plath made the transition is nowhere more apparent than in 'The Bee Meeting', written in the autumn of 1962. The occasion is a simple one; village friends take the poet to watch a suitably protected expert move the virgin bees from the queen bee, for there is to be no killing that year. Transmuted into poetry the experience becomes a metaphor of isolation. The villagers are depersonalised by their protective clothing and the poet, vulnerable in her sleeveless summer dress, feels herself to be an outsider: 'I am nude as a chicken neck, does nobody love me?' Eventually she is given a smock which covers her arms and neck and she also hopes that it will disguise her fear. The party then moves off through the beanfields to the grove where the hives are kept. The beanfields are beautiful but menacing; the feathery delicacy of the leaves being offset by the dangerous vitality of the scarlet flowers. When they reach the grove the poet dons a hat and veil and feels that this completes a sort of initiation ceremony: 'They are making me one of them.' The imagery is of sterility hospitals and illness and she feels that the situation she is about to be plunged into is a momentous one. Her feelings are those of someone caught in a nightmare for she is rooted to the spot and cannot escape, indeed there is no place of escape for 'I could not run without having to run forever'. As the hive is opened and the villagers search for the queen bee the poet stands aside feeling both fear and sympathy. She wants to become a 'personage in a hedge-row' so that no one will notice her and she will suffer no hostility but she also feels sympathy for the old queen bee, forced to live for another year before the release of 'the bride flight/The upflight of the murderess into a heaven that loves her'. At the end of the poem life has been preserved; the virgin bees are left to dream for another year of a duel one of them must inevitably win, but the queen bee does not appear; she is not grateful. The poet feels even more isolated now; she sees the protection of life in terms of the coldness of death: 'Whose is that long white box in the grove, what have they accomplished, why am I cold?' The whole sequence of bee poems, written in the autumn of 1962, is a con-tinuing drama in which the precise technical details are a mask for the naked suffering of the poet.

The majority of the poems in *Ariel* reflect an inner, personal world. Three which combine the private with the public are 'Daddy', 'Fever 103º' and 'Lady Lazarus'; these poems also belong to autumn, 1962. Sylvia Plath writes in all three poems of her feelings about the concentration camps and the bombing of Hiroshima in conjunction with her inner pain. The most remark-able of the three is 'Daddy'. The poem has already received a good deal of critical attention which has focused on the autobiograph-aspect. The danger of such criticism lies in its assumption that the poem is objectively 'true', that it bears a precise relationship to the facts of the poet's life. Without a doubt this poem embodies most forcefully the feeling which runs through her later poetry that the distress she suffered was in some way connected with her mem-ories of her dead father, but the poem cannot be literally or historically true. Otto Plath, who was born in 1885 and came to America at the age of fifteen, died when his daughter was nine and certainly could not have been the active German Nazi officer of the poem. However he was of pure Prussian descent and one of his daughter's obsessions was that, given other circumstances, it might have been that he would have become a Nazi. In the same way her mother, Aurelia Plath, who is of Austrian descent, could have had Jewish blood and if she had lived in Europe might have become one of the host of murdered Jews. In terms of the poem itself the mother figure is unimportant; the daughter appropriates the mother's attributes and the relationship is developed through the father–daughter, Nazi–Jew complexity. Questioned about this poem by Peter Orr, Sylvia Plath explained:[4]

> In particular my background is, may I say, German and Austrian. On one side I am first generation American, on one side I am second generation American, and so my concern with concentration camps and so on is uniquely intense. And then, again, I'm rather a political person as well, so I suppose that's part of what it comes from.

When she described the poem at another time she did so in dramatic terms which included no overt hint that the situation described was her own:[5]

> The poem is spoken by a girl with an Electra complex. Her father died while she thought he was God. Her case is complicated by the fact that her father was also a Nazi and her mother very possibly part-Jewish. In the daughter the two strains marry and paralyse each other—she has to act out the awful little allegory before she is free of it.

The poem exploits Freudian psychology which argues that the child is, at some stages in its development, 'in love' with the parent. The girl reacts with hate for the father who has made her suffer by dying at such a point in her development. The description of the father as 'marble-heavy' and a 'ghastly statue' reveals the ambivalence of her attitude for he is also associated with the

4. Orr, *op. cit.*, p. 169.

5. Quoted in a poetry broadsheet issued by the *Critical Quarterly* Society in 1964.

beauty of the sea. The image of the father as a statue echoes the similar conception of 'The Colossus'; here, as in the earlier poem, the statue is of huge and awesome proportions. The ambivalent feelings of fear and love have remained with the daughter as an obsession which dwarfs and restricts her own life, and in an attempt to rid herself of it she must ritually destroy the memory of the father:

> Daddy, I have had to kill you.
> You died before I had time—
> Marble-heavy, a bag full of God,

She first attempted to do this by joining the father through suicide, but then found an escape through marriage to a man with many of the father's characteristics:

> And then I knew what to do.
> I made a model of you,
> A man in black with a Meinkampf look
>
> And a love of the rack and the screw.
> And I said I do, I do.

The psychological is only one aspect of the poem however. Sylvia Plath extends the reference by making the father a German Nazi and the girl a Jew, so that on a historical and actual, as well as on an emotional level their relationship is that of torturer and tortured. The boot image of the first verse can now be seen not only as an effective image for the obsessional nature of the daughter's neurosis, but also as carrying suggestions of the brutality associated with the father as Nazi officer. The transition from the father–daughter to the Nazi–Jew relationship is simply and dramatically effected. The hatred of the daughter merges into the emotional paralysis of her recognition, as Jew, of him as Nazi: 'I never could talk to you./The tongue stuck in my jaw.' The jaw becomes the barbed wire of the concentration camps, and the repeated self-assertive 'Ich' of the German language recalls the sound of the engines carrying Jews to the camps. In revolt from the obscenity of the language—which is an extension of the emotional revolt against the father—the daughter begins to talk like a Jew, that is she identifies herself with the archetypal, suffering Jew of the camps. She now describes the father as a Nazi officer and no longer associates him with God but with a swastika 'So black no sky could squeak through'. The theme of inter-mingled love and hate arises again as the daughter comments on the sexual fascination of cruelty:

> Every woman adores a Fascist,
> The boot in the face, the brute
> Brute heart of a brute like you.

It finds a further echo in the description of the husband who is also 'A man in black with a Meinkampf look', who has been chosen for his similarity to the father in the hope that his presence will exorcise the daughter's obsession.

A. Alvarez recalls that Sylvia Plath described this poem as 'light verse':[6]

> When she first read me this poem a few days after she wrote it, she called it a piece of 'light verse'. It obviously isn't, yet equally obviously it also isn't the racking personal confession that a mere description or précis of it might make it sound.

The significance of such a term applied to 'Daddy' becomes clearer if we consider the theory of light verse held by W. H. Auden. Auden has written:[7]

> Light verse can be serious. It has only come to mean vers de société, Triolets, smoke-room limericks, because under the social conditions which produced the Romantic Revival, and which have persisted, more or less, ever since, it has only been in trivial matters that poets have felt in sufficient intimacy with their audience to be able to forget themselves and their singing-robes.

6. Alvarez, *op. cit.*, p. 66.
7. Introduction to *The Oxford Book of Light Verse*, ed. W. H. Auden, 1938.

Auden equates the writing of 'light verse' with a homogeneous and slowly changing society in which the interests and perceptions of most men are similar; difficult poetry is produced in an unstable society from which the poet feels detached. Undoubtedly, at the time of writing, Auden saw himself as belonging to an unstable society, and his use of 'light verse' is highly sophisticated in that he consciously adopted it as a means of communication for his social criticism; it is not, according to Auden, the natural way in which any modern poet would express himself. 'Daddy' may reasonably be said to be 'light' in the sense that Auden's early poetry is 'light'. This quality is purely an attribute of form and does not in any way characterise the subject which is fully serious. The strong, simple rhythm, the full rhymes and subtle half-rhymes, the repetitive, incantatory vowel-sounds sweep the poem along in a jaunty approximation to a ballad. The mood of the poem is conversational, the daughter directly addresses the memory of the father with energy and feeling. The vocabulary is simple, the last line seeming almost too indulgently colloquial until we realise that the strategy of the whole poem has been to undermine emotion. When Sylvia Plath described this poem as 'a piece of light verse' she was focusing our attention on the flippant, choppy, conversational swing of the poem which, with its dramatic structure, gives a measure of impersonality to a subject which, less surely handled, could have been destroyed by either self-pity or sensationalism.

A companion piece to 'Daddy', in which the poet again fuses the worlds of personal pain and corporate suffering, is 'Lady Lazarus'. In this poem a disturbing tension is established between the seriousness of the experience described and the misleadingly light form of the poem. The vocabulary and rhythms which approximate to the colloquial simplicity of conversational speech, the frequently end-stopped lines, the repetitions which have the effect of mockingly counteracting the violence of the meaning, all establish the deliberately flippant note which this poem strives to achieve. These are all devices which also operate in Auden's 'light verse', but the constantly shifting tone of 'Lady Lazarus' is found less frequently in Auden's more cerebral poetry. At times the tone is hysterically strident and demanding:

The peanut-crunching crowd
Shoves in to see

Them unwrap me hand and foot—
The big strip tease.
Gentlemen, ladies

These are my hands
My knees.

Then it modulates into a calmer irony as the persona mocks herself for her pretensions to tragedy: 'Dying/Is an art, like everything else./I do it exceptionally well.' As in 'Daddy' Sylvia Plath has used a limited amount of autobiographical detail in this poem; the references to suicide in 'Lady Lazarus' reflect her own experience. As in 'Daddy', however, the personal element is subordinate to a much more inclusive dramatic structure, and one answer to those critics who have seen her work as merely confessional is that she used her personal and painful material as a way of entering into and illustrating much wider themes and subjects. In 'Lady Lazarus' the poet again equates her suffering with the experiences of the tortured Jews, she becomes, as a result of the suicide she inflicts on herself, a Jew:

A sort of walking miracle, my skin
Bright as a Nazi lampshade,
My right foot

A paperweight,
My face a featureless, fine
Jew linen.

The reaction of the crowd who push in with morbid interest to see the saved suicide mimics the attitude of many to the revelations of the concentration camps; there is a brutal insistence on the pain which many apparently manage to see with scientific detachment. 'Lady Lazarus' represents an extreme use of the 'light verse' technique. Auden never forced such grotesque material into such an insistently jaunty poem, and the anger and compassion which inform the poem are rarely found so explicitly in his work. 'Lady Lazarus' is also a supreme example of Sylvia Plath's skill as an artist. She takes very personal, painful material and controls and forms it with the utmost rigour into a highly wrought poem, which is partly effective because of the polar opposition between the terrible gaiety of its form and the fiercely uncompromising seriousness of its subject. If we categorise a poem such as 'Lady Lazarus' as 'confessional' or 'extremist' then we highlight only one of its elements. It is also a poem of social criticism with a strong didactic intent, and a work of art which reveals great technical and intellectual ability. The hysteria is intentional and effective.

In *Ariel* the hesitant, too-controlled gestures of *The Colossus* have disappeared, to be replaced by a freer, surer poetry; the underlying dynamic of which is the attempt to relate and harmonise the internal experience with the perceived external events. The uneasy apprehensions of the earlier poems have developed into a systematic laying bare of the terrible discrepancy between actuality and desire. This dichotomy is operative in both the spiritual and the material. In 'Lady Lazarus' the worlds of war and religion are opposed and contrasted through the ironic reference of the title. In 'The Couriers' Sylvia Plath comments bitterly on the gulf between the promise of marriage and its disillusionments. In 'Little Fugue' she is depressed by the utter helplessness of the maimed human being in the face of an uncaring and implacable destiny, whose main weapon is the very imperfection of man:

> The yew's black fingers wag;
> Cold clouds go over.
> So the deaf and dumb
> Signal the blind, and are ignored.

In one of her last poems, 'Kindness', she dwells on the futility of the normal human gesture. In 'Eavesdropper', an uncollected late poem,[8] disillusion with marriage has become an almost Swiftian excoriation:

> . . . a desert of cow-people
> Trundling their udders home
> To the electric milker, the wifey,

8. 'Eavesdropper, *Poetry*, 102, 1963, p. 296.

> The big blue eye
> That watches, like God, or the sky
> The ciphers that watch it.

However the tone is infrequently satirical. For the satirist the act of writing is, in itself, a positive attempt to cure the ills it seeks to expose; Sylvia Plath saw no end to the blackness of her world.

'Getting There', one of the most openly anguished poems, sees the progress of living as the journey of a train carrying wounded soldiers, mutilated, bleeding, despairing, yet still surviving, towards a death which offers the only possibility of peace:

> It is a trainstop, the nurses
> Undergoing the faucet water, its veils, veils in a
>   nunnery,
> Touching their wounded,
> The men the blood still pumps forward,
> Legs, arms piled outside
> The tent of unending cries—
> A hospital of dolls.

Living contains only blood, suffering, pain, wars and screaming; the persona can find no moment of peace or rest which does not resolve itself into the depressed, dumb 'Stasis in darkness' of 'Ariel'. The reference to Eliot is obvious in the lines:

> Is there no still place
> Turning and turning in the middle air,
> Untouched and untouchable.

However the only stillness which the traveller of 'Getting There' can hope for is in the complete immobility of death, disturbingly seen as a birth into purity:

> The carriages rock, they are cradles.
> And I stepping from this skin
> Of old bandages, boredoms, old faces
>
> Step to you from the black car of Lethe,
> Pure as a baby.

In the poems written in the last week of her life Sylvia Plath moved away from an anguished contemplation of the suffering of living to a concentration on the peace of death. 'Edge' has as its subject the suicide which must have been much in her mind in these last days. Death is perfection, it is beautiful and noble; the dead body has the dignity of a piece of classical Greek statuary—a conception which also appears in the description of the dead children in an earlier poem 'Death and Co.'. The dead children in 'Edge' have been folded back into the mother's body protectively, as the ultimate loving gesture, similar to the natural folding of the rose around itself in the face of oncoming night in the garden. The imagery of war and disease which invades many of the earlier *Ariel* poems is replaced by an exquisitely lyrical natural imagery:

> She has folded
>
> Them back into her body as petals
> Of a rose close when the garden
>
> Stiffens and odours bleed
> From the sweet, deep throats of the night flower.

The tone of the poet, now celebrating death with no revulsion, has changed entirely from the tone of stanza four of 'Berck-Plage'. There the death of the old man was felt to be grotesque: 'This is what it is to be complete. It is horrible.' The moon, which throughout the poetry represents a world of unrelieved suffering, is not saddened by the deaths she beholds; they are a natural part of her domain. The poet accepts that it is only by stepping over the edge and into death that she can defeat the world of the moon, which in life has oppressed her.

The ability to write about death with control, almost with objectivity, or rather the ability to make in the process of artistic creation the most subjective feelings acquire a certain appearance of reasoned and reasonable objectivity, is one of the most remarkable qualities which Sylvia Plath's last poetry exhibits. 'Contusion', 'Kindness' and 'Words', which were also written in the last week of her life, are all devoid of the passionate intensity, the near hysteria of the earlier poems. The most basic opposition which she explored in *Ariel* was that between life and death and she resolves this opposition in favour of death in these poems. The jerky, tortured style of the earlier poems, which were in terrified revolt against the forces of blackness and death has given way to a more measured simplicity. 'Contusion', one of these late poems, is developed through a series of ordered statements, which are all images of death, and which culminate in a verse which underlines the significance of the mirror as a symbol in Sylvia Plath's work:

> The heart shuts,
> The sea slides back,
> The mirrors are sheeted.

6   *The Bell Jar*

Sylvia Plath's only novel, *The Bell Jar*, analyses the adolescent struggle in its final crisis in the life of a nineteen year old American university student from Boston. It describes the conflict which develops in and finally disrupts Esther Greenwood's mind as she faces the necessity for emerging from the sheltering world of school and university to enter an adult world which makes much more complex demands on her. Her intellectual ability, which has identified her in the academic world, is counterbalanced by a lack of social experience or ease, and her desire for sophistication leads her half-unwillingly into a series of disastrous social and sexual encounters. The first nine chapters outline the reactions and dilemmas of the sheltered middle-class girl released for the first time into the wilderness of city life; the remaining eleven describe her growing inability to take decisions, which culminates in an unsuccessful suicide attempt, followed by hospital treatment and eventual recovery. The novel has a tri-partite structure and the construction of the second and third parts differs from that of the first. The first nine chapters set the scene, introduce the major characters and indicate the basic conflicts by interspersing the narrative present with episodes drawn from Esther's past. However once the conflicts have been established and as the bell jar descends the development of the novel is concentrated in the narrative present which continues almost uninterrupted to the end of the novel, encompassing both the second and third sections. Chapters ten to thirteen form the second section, chapters fourteen to twenty the third.

Section one ends with an episode which is both the symbolic and the narrative heart of the novel. After the finally disastrous encounter with the woman-hater, Marco, Esther throws away all the expensive clothes which she had bought specially for the month in New York and which have represented her desire for social sophistication. This action marks the end of the New York episode where the protagonist's sanity has been precariously maintained and signals the beginning of breakdown as Esther returns to the claustrophobia of suburban Boston and the prospect of a summer spent with the mother to whom she is so antagonistic. Symbolically it indicates the end of Esther's attempts to achieve social integration and sexual experience and a cremation image fittingly describes the falling clothes.

The second and shortest section ends in the attempted suicide towards which Esther has inexorably moved after her return to Boston. Sylvia Plath employs an image of oblivion and peace here:

> The silence drew off, baring the pebbles and shells and all the tatty wreckage of my life. Then, at the rim of vision, it gathered itself, and in one sweeping tide, rushed me to sleep.

The third section is concerned with recovery and rehabilitation and the novel rather tantalisingly ends as Esther enters the room for the final interview with the board of doctors who will pronounce her fit to return to college:

> The eyes and faces all turned themselves towards me, and guiding myself by them, as by a magical thread, I stepped into the room.

In New York Esther finds herself unable to organise her different ambitions into any coherent aims. She sees a divergence between the world of intellectual and artistic aspiration and that of society which cannot be bridged by any working compromise. The related themes of academic and social achievement, and the necessity of combining them in a proportion acceptable to the individual, are organised through the creation of compared and contrasted characters who represent certain compromises made between society and self. In the first section of the novel Esther relates herself to three female characters—Doreen, Betsy and Jay Cee. Doreen and Betsy are both college girls who have also won prizes on the magazine on which Esther works. Esther sees Doreen as sharply sophisticated, socially experienced, unacademic but clever, and is fascinated by Doreen's freedom, which she recognises as an internal quality of thought and attitude. Betsy is sweet and kind, totally unintellectual and she finally achieves fame as a cover-girl; Esther envies her normality and her ability to accept her femininity. Jay Cee, the literary editor of the fashion magazine and Esther's boss for the month, is a successful career woman who has made a working compromise between marriage and ambition, although Esther is typically unable to imagine that any private and specifically sexual activity lies behind her efficient public persona. Esther feels that Jay Cee offers her wisdom while Betsy offers her safety, but she prefers the possibility of experience suggested by Doreen, whose presence gives her the confidence she would normally lack: 'being with Doreen made me forget all my worries. I felt wise and cynical as all hell.' However during the funny, but for Esther disastrous, episode of Doreen's encounter with Lenny she admits to herself that admiration for Doreen does not extend to the ability to emulate.

Esther sees Jay Cee as a symbol of the worldly success she would like to attain herself and is forced by Jay Cee's insistence that she take full advantage of her opportunities on the magazine, to reappraise her ambitions. During a chilling interview with Jay Cee she realises that the academic and artistic career she has in fantasy created for herself provides no antidote to her growing sense of isolation; her previous glib answers to the question: 'What are you going to do?' are no longer applicable. Esther's lack of self-knowledge makes her seek identification with others, but just as she was unable to join Betsy in innocent, if unambitious enjoyment, so she is unable to accept Jay Cee's practical advice and she retreats into a fantasy world in which she surprises Jay Cee with her artistic ability. On her last night in New York she allows Doreen to persuade her to go to the country club dance, where her encounter with Marco forms the most ignominious of her social experiences to date. She leaves New York the next day in a state of complete disillusion and depression, symbolised by the oddity of her appearance—having discarded all her own clothes she is dressed in a skirt and blouse of Betsy's and has deliberately not washed away the smears of blood which Marco left on her face.

However it is against the attitudes to femininity dominant in her social background that Esther revolts most strongly. These attitudes are concentrated in the character of Mrs Willard, the mother of Esther's rejected boyfriend Buddy, but they are also attributed to her mother and grandmother who are friendly with the Willards and approve of Buddy. An intelligent woman who spends her life being an efficient wife and mother, Mrs Willard is quoted by Buddy as saying:

> 'What a man wants is a mate and what a woman wants is infinite security' and 'What a man is is an arrow into the future and what a woman is is the place the arrow shoots off from.'

Esther refuses to accept this statement of female needs because it disregards the possibility of personal distinction for a woman. Dodo Conway exemplifies a superficially similar position but Esther feels unwilling interest in Dodo because she has made a virtue out of the female role and is supremely happy. Although Esther recognises the strength of Dodo's position her final reaction is a determined if defensive negative: 'Children make me sick.' Nevertheless the generosity and personal fulfilment of Dodo's fertility differs radically from Mrs Willard's position, which Esther finally recognises as a repressive maternal domination, in which the submission of the female to the male is merely a rationalisation of exactly the opposite situation:

> I had a picture of Mrs Willard with her heather-mixture tweeds and her sensible shoes and her wise, maternal maxims. Mr Willard was her little boy, and his voice was high and clear, like a little boy's.

However beneath the feminist level the novel more importantly explores the stresses and conflicts which arise in the personality of the artist whose vision is a betrayal of the society in which he lives. In the past, we are told, Esther has found identity in the world of organised intellectual effort, but when the loss of intellectual direction which she has discovered in herself under the stress of Jay Cee's questioning is augmented by her discovery that she has not gained a place on the summer creative writing course, her world quickly disintegrates. For a short time she tries to write a novel, to learn shorthand, to begin her English honours' dissertation on twin images in Joyce, but eventually she relinquishes all efforts and succumbs to the mental inertia which ends in breakdown, appropriately revealed to her in her inability to read or write. Significantly what she sees as her rejection by the world of the intellect is accompanied by the savagery of her refusal of the social world in her final rejection of Buddy Willard, whom she now sees as a hypocrite because of his conformity to an external social code which many of his actions do not support. Esther's revolt against him is also part of her revolt against her family, who think Buddy very eligible because he seems to fulfil their expectations. Esther at first welcomed Buddy as a suitor, partly for himself and partly because he releases her from the teasing of her college-mates—it is emphasised in *The Bell Jar* that Esther is an outsider in the life of the university even though her intellectual prowess provides her with a sense of identity.

It is when the intellectual world fails her and she attempts to reject the social world which she sees as merely an accepted code of hollow attitudes and assumptions that breakdown occurs. She can neither tolerate nor rationalise the rift which she sees between the accepted world, which is a predominantly false one, and the bleakness of her own world of the bell jar. The crisis is now deeper than that of adolescence for it is the struggle of the artist to accept and live with his vision, while still existing within the society in which he feels himself to be an outsider. Recovery lies in the acceptance of the differences between the external world and that revealed by the creative insight. The attitudes of those outside the bell jar have not changed, the artist must accept that his internal world may be more real to him than that common world of actions and events, 'telegrams and anger', which he shares with those who see his vision as an illness:

> I remembered the cadavers and Doreen and the story of the fig-tree and Marco's diamond and the sailor on

the Common and Doctor Gordon's wall-eyed nurse
and the broken thermometers and the negro with his
two kinds of beans and the twenty pounds I gained on
insulin and the rock that bulged between sky and sea
like a grey skull.

Maybe forgetfulness, like a kind snow, should numb
and cover them. But they were part of me. They were
my landscape.

The mode of communication between author and reader of
The Bell Jar is that of invited self-identification with the protagonist; the major difficulty which this entails lies in the provision
of any degree of objectivity against which the subjective world
can be measured. Sylvia Plath has been able to introduce some
degree of such objectivity into the novel by endowing Esther with
a wryly self-mocking sense of humour which, although it does not
save her, serves both as a sense of proportion and perception.
Ironic humour as a means of perception modulates the subjective
world of the bell jar and Esther's ability to stand outside herself
and comment on her environment allows the reader to appreciate
the subjective world more fully, for it provides the necessary link
between the worlds of common and individual experience. Further
dimension is added to the novel by the imagery, which is consist-
ent and pervasive enough to be regarded as a principle of unity
and which both concentrates and extends Esther's dilemma. The
symbolic title indicates the nature of the prose, which seeks to
combine narrative immediacy with the creation of a more,
subjective, internal world through the use of imagery of alienation
and inadequacy. The bell jar itself is the symbol of the inner,
alienated world:

> Wherever I sat—on the deck of a ship or at a street
> café in Paris or Bangkok—I would be sitting under the
> same glass bell jar, stewing in my own sour air.

After Esther's first experience of E.C.T. the suffocating oppression
of the bell jar lightens and she feels some degree of relief. Recovery
brings escape from the bell jar although it does not remove its
threat:

> All the heat and fear had purged itself. I felt
> surprisingly at peace. The bell jar hung suspended, a
> few feet above my head. I was open to the circulating
> air.

One pervasive thread of imagery is that concerned with death which is introduced on the first page of the novel:

> It was like the first time I saw a cadaver. For weeks
> afterwards, the cadaver's head—or what was left of it
> —floated up behind my eggs and bacon at breakfast
> and behind the face of Buddy Willard, who was
> responsible for my seeing it in the first place, and
> pretty soon I felt as though I was carrying that
> cadaver's head around with me on a string, like some
> black, noseless balloon stinking of vinegar.

The image has a threefold effect; firstly it establishes the subjective condition of Esther's mind, secondly it foreshadows the hospital episode and introduces Buddy Willard, and thirdly it indicates that the final culmination of Esther's disturbance will be an attempt to fuse her identity with that of the real corpse she saw in the hospital and the metaphorical corpse which has become a part of her world. Sylvia Plath constantly translates Esther's experience in the narrative present episodes into images of her inner journey; she recreates the mechanics of the mind which perceives, reacts and symbolises.

Death imagery appears importantly at the end of chapter nine in the episode already referred to where Esther flings her clothes from the hotel roof top, an action which symbolises her refusal to enter the publishing world or the social one, and her deliberate relinquishing of herself to the mental death in which she is increasingly caught. The funereal city refuses the gesture of offered truce and the clothes float down into the dark heart of the city:

> A white flake floated out into the night, and began
> its slow descent. I wondered on what street or roof top
> it would come to rest.

> I tugged at the bundle again.
> The wind made an effort, but failed,
> and a batlike shadow sank towards the roof garden of
> the penthouse opposite.
> Piece by piece, I fed my
> wardrobe to the night wind, and flutteringly like a
> loved one's ashes, the grey scraps were ferried off, to
> settle here, there, exactly where I would never know,
> in the dark heart of New York.

On one level the passage is an exact recreation of a particular scene, treated with a certain amount of ironic humour—but the key words accumulate—failed, batlike, shadow, sank, ashes, grey, dark—and we are led into the subjective centre of Esther's inexorably darkening mind. Such are the overtones of the passage that the reader who is paying particular attention to the imagery comes to see the very failure of the wind to carry the clothes upwards as a symbolic correspondence to Esther's failure to escape from her own dark night.

The largest imagistic complex in *The Bell Jar* expresses Esther's feelings of inadequacy and alienation. These images are concentrated very densely up to the end of chapter thirteen—that is throughout the first two sections of the book. Several of them are centred on ideas of movement or progression. Esther's emotional progress is essentially directionless and beyond her control and her actual physical movement around New York becomes an image to describe her mental condition:

> Only I wasn't steering anything, not even myself. I
> just bumped from hotel to work and to parties and
> from parties to my hotel and back to work like a
> trolley-bus.

Any progression which she achieves must be in the wrong direction, taking her not towards integration and self-acceptance but further into the wilderness of isolation; as she watches Lenny and Doreen jiving she is assailed by the sense of rushing very rapidly away from the normal world of personal relationships. Decisive movement when it is achieved in the ski-ing episode becomes a return to the comfort of the womb, a further method of escape rather than of acceptance or the attempt to accept, although it does contain some suggestion that Esther is beginning to search out the basic conflicts and to reach down into the core of herself to find her most secret fears and compulsions:

> I plummeted down past the zigzaggers, the students, the experts, through year after year of doubleness and smiles and compromise, into my own past.
> People and trees receded on either hand like the dark sides of a tunnel as I hurtled on to the still, bright point at the end of it, the pebble at the bottom of the well, the white sweet baby cradled in its mother's belly.

The figures she moves through on her downhill flight are both the actual skiers and representational references to the fellow students who have achieved compromise, and the experts who have tried to teach her something; she rejects all this in favour of an uncompromising return to the root of her being, an attempt to know herself shorn of all the social and intellectual hypocrisy she has noted in others.

The movement imagery becomes increasingly desolate as Esther's depression deepens; when she hears of her failure to gain a place on the creative writing course she sees herself helplessly falling to disaster. Eventually she arrives at a position from which progression is impossible because the future is an unreadable blank and the present contains no motive for progression. The images of static despair accumulate to the end of chapter thirteen with its attempted suicide. They are not replaced in the final section of the novel by images of accepted direction and knowledge because the novel ends with Esther just recovering, and thus the earlier subjective world has not yet been replaced by a newer, more healthy one. In fact, in one sense, recovery for Esther Greenwood lies in the ability to replace the old imaginative activity with a rational and common sense attitude which denies the artist's insights into a world beyond the world.

Another major group of images is concerned with Esther's sense of the impending disaster which presses in on her, accompanied by a perception of the world as a hostile place in which she is losing any sense of individuality. The inability to make any choice or decision produces a feeling of sterility and the protagonist views her life as a fig-tree; every fig offers a different solution, a different offer of fame or happiness, but she is unable to choose and as she hesitates the opportunity is lost, the figs wither and fall. Marriage would be no answer to the loss of identity because Esther views it as the final loss of independence and Sylvia Plath incorporates a startling political image to describe the condition of being married for women: 'when you were married and had children it was like being brainwashed, and afterwards you went about numb as a slave in some private, totalitarian state'. This image is a reminder of the political awareness that dominates many of the late poems.

The hostility of the outer world becomes an active menace which Esther feels surrounding her, pushing her into final numbness seen as a 'black airless sack with no way out'. The description of the act of suicide as being pushed into a sack is paralleled in 'Daddy': 'But they pulled me out of the sack,/And they stuck me together with glue.' As the crisis approaches Esther's vision darkens and she begins to see her surroundings in terms of a distorted animal world in which people are worms. The image recurs when she recovers consciousness in hospital and worms also figure in the experience of recovery as it is seen in 'Lady Lazarus': 'They had to call and call/And pick the worms off me like sticky pearls.' The images describing her awakening in hospital in *The Bell Jar* are closely similar to the imagery of 'The Stones', the seventh part of 'Poem For a Birthday'. The novel and the poem both embody images of physical repairing.

Imagery is used in *The Bell Jar* to develop and communicate the inner, subjective world in contrast to the external world which is presented in the narrative present episodes. After the suicide attempt the imagery becomes less dense as the novel moves increasingly into the narrative present and the objective world of health begins to replace the world of the bell jar. Superficially the comparative simplicity of the third section may seem to indicate a reduction in the skill of the author, but the extension of the imagistic world would have necessitated the development of the novel beyond its actual theme. The process of recovery is the replacement of the inner, alienated world by an objective world of communication and perception, and as the novel ends with Esther about to leave the hospital it would not have been feasible within the framework of the novel to have developed a new subjective world to replace the earlier world of growing insanity.

Sylvia Plath had written short stories as an adolescent and had had some published as a student, others have been published posthumously. *The Bell Jar* is her only published novel. It is interesting to speculate on why she turned to the novel at this stage in her development. One aspect of the later poetry is the attempt to come to terms with personal experience of the most painful kind; the personality struggles to define itself through words, shaping and making explicit the most indistinct and complex of experiences; the artist creates, in part, from self-knowledge. We do not really need Anne Sexton's testimony[1] to understand that *The Bell Jar* is largely autobiographical. The comparisons between Sylvia Plath's own family background, education and interests and those of Esther Greenwood are too great to be coincidental, but just as the poetry is more than therapeutic, so the novel cannot be dismissed as merely autobiographical.

Sylvia Plath's later poetry and her enthusiastic acclaim for the poetry of Robert Lowell and Anne Sexton indicate that autobiography was not material which she saw as being intrinsically unsuited to poetry, so her motive for turning to the novel was not just to come to terms with personal experience of a particularly scarring kind—she had already written about the experience of breakdown in 'Poem For a Birthday'. In an interview with Peter Orr[2] she indicated her conception of the novel as a form which can include much more of the circumstantial detail of daily living than is possible in the more compressed medium of poetry:

> I feel that in a novel, for example, you can get in toothbrushes and all the paraphernalia that one finds in daily life, and I find this more difficult in poetry. Poetry, I feel, is a tyrannical discipline, you've got to go so far, so fast, in such a small space that you've just got to turn away all the peripherals. And I miss them!

1. Sexton, *op. cit.* p. 175
2. Orr, *op. cit.*, p. 171.

> I'm a woman, I like my little Lares and Penates, I like
> trivia, and I find that in a novel I can get more of life,
> perhaps not such an intense life, but certainly more of
> life, and so I've become very interested in novel
> writing as a result.

This statement is very revealing in relation to *The Bell Jar*, where
we find both the insights into mental and emotional conditions
of *Ariel* and *Winter Trees* mainly conveyed through the imagery
and a more external social comment on certain aspects of the
America of the mid-fifties. Esther's comments on her surroundings
project a vision of a society which is very similar to that developed
in the novels of Saul Bellow, where the intellectual liberal is lost
in the modern, uncaring, commercial society. New York has
'mystery and magnificence' for Esther but it is also hostile and
impersonal:

> Mirage-grey at the bottom of their granite canyons the
> hot streets wavered in the sun, the car tops sizzled and
> glittered, and the dry, cindery dust blew into my eyes
> and down my throat.

Doreen survives in this society because she is hard enough, Betsy
because she is uninvolved with it and Jay Cee because she has
conquered it through success. Esther fails because she has not
learnt, or refuses to apply, the rules for survival. Suburban
Boston is gossipy, claustrophobic and uniform, and the two
alternative ways of living within such an environment—conformity, which is adopted by Mrs Willard and Mrs Greenwood, or a
complete indifference to external social mores, which is Dodo
Conway's reaction—are both rejected by Esther, who sees the
unending, neatly arranged sameness of the living areas of middle-
class society as a stifling oppression.

Esther is torn between her perceptions of the society in which
she lives as artificial and hypocritical and her desire to attain one-
ness with this society, and in the hospital, for a time, her attitude
exactly parallels the attitude she has earlier exhibited to her
college environment. In both situations she is an outsider unable
to defend herself because she still seeks unity. One mark of her

recovery is her ability to recognise the inane, undirected silliness of the behaviour of the very women she had earlier envied; she is acquiring the necessary strength to live with her moral and ethical judgments, even though they reveal to her a society in which she feels alien. As an autobiographical document, a record of some of the stresses which drove her to suicide *The Bell Jar* is of the utmost importance to any student of Sylvia Plath, but it is even more important as a catalogue of some of the insights she had into the America of the fifties. An American by birth and upbringing but with strong European connections Sylvia Plath admitted to Peter Orr that her sympathies lay with the America of the past rather than the present:[3]

> Well, I think that as far as language goes I'm an American, I'm afraid, my accent is American, my way of talk is an American way of talk, I'm an old-fashioned American. That's probably one of the reasons why I'm in England now and why I'll always stay in England.

3. *Ibid.*, p. 168.

7   *Imagery*

The recurrence of interrelated symbols and image clusters is one
of the unifying elements of Sylvia Plath's poetry. In the later work
the repeated appearance of certain central images and symbols,
such as the moon, candles, mirrors, clouds, statues, trains, yew
trees, forms a substantial substructure from which the individual
poems are developed. A survey of her work demonstrates the
progression from the largely denotive significance of words in her
early poetry to their referential value in her later poetry. Words
such as 'moon', 'bald', 'blue', acquire such connotative richness
that they become concentrated allusions to associations and
references beyond the immediate range of the individual poem.
However to analyse in detail the symbolism and imagery would
be a major study in itself; consequently this chapter will concen-
trate on a study of the meanings associated with Sylvia Plath's use
of the word 'moon', perhaps the central symbol of her work, and
those symbols and images most frequently associated with the
moon.

The word occurs in the early poetry either as a hyphenated
compound with adjectival value: 'moon-struck', 'moon-bound',
'moon-blued', 'moon-white', 'moon-glint', or as the related
adjective 'moony'. The moon appears in one of the earliest
poems, 'A Mad Girl's Love Song',[1] with a self-explanatory and
fairly conventional proverbial meaning of insane: 'I dreamed that
you bewitched me into bed/And sung me moon-struck, kissed me
quite insane'. However the use of 'moon' or 'moony' as an adjective describing human beings appears in several other poems,
acquiring a more complex value as the work develops. The
students of 'Watercolour of Grantchester Meadows' are in a
'moony indolence of love'; the word's primary meaning here is
associated with that of 'A Mad Girl's Love Song', that is a

1. 'A Mad Girl's Love Song'. *Mademoiselle*, August 1953, p. 358.

temporary blindness induced by love, but the context of the poem suggests a further meaning; the self-absorption of the lovers has blinded them to the crueler realities symbolised by the predatory savagery of the rat and owl, and by association 'moony' now acquires some suggestion of unrealistic or inattentive.

The moon is frequently associated with the sea, both in the early and the later work. The first major statement of this relationship can be found in 'Hardcastle Crags', where Sylvia Plath defines the dominance of the moon even over the sea, which so frequently represents freedom to her:

> . . . the incessant seethe of grasses,
> Riding in the full
>
> Of the moon, manes to the wind,
> Tireless, tied, as a moon-bound sea
> Moves on its root.

In the later poems also the sea becomes an element subdued to the painful domination of an uncaring moon: 'As the moon for its ivory powders, scours the sea', 'It drags the sea after it like a dark crime', 'It is she that drags the blood-black sea around'. In the last quotation the poet begins to develop the relationship between the moon, the sea and the menstrual cycle which she states more openly in the last poems.

The moon is always part of the otherworld of internal experience and in 'The Ghost's Leavetaking', 'The Thin People' and 'Maudlin' it is associated with a world of dreams, nursery rhymes and fairy tales—although there are also other important associations in 'Maudlin'. These poems reinforce the growing significance of the moon as a concrete representation of the strange, magical world which is in many ways opposed to the earthly reality, and which is ultimately to resolve itself into the otherworld of death. These connotations of strangeness are rarely desirable or attractive. In 'Two View of a Cadaver Room' 'moon', used as a verb, defines the limpidity of pickled foetuses: 'In their jars the snail-nosed babies moon and glow.' Similar imagery appears in *The Bell Jar* when Esther visits the hospital with Buddy, who shows her a series of glass jars containing foetuses preserved at various stages in their growth. In 'Departure' the moon is part of a hostilely metallic world which rejects the poet absolutely:

> Retrospect shall not soften such penury—
> Sun's brass, the moon's steely patinas,
> The leaden slag of the world.

The use of the moon in the early poetry is basically denotive and largely unremarkable. The word begins to acquire a much greater complexity and significance in 'Moonrise'. The poem develops from visual, concrete images of whiteness to a consideration of the spiritual suggestions of the colour. The poet formulates an opposition between white, which is the colour of the moon, of death, decay, infertility and redness, the colour of ripeness, maturity and life. Images of fertility accompany the change from white to red, while compelling images of death and decay are related to whiteness: 'White catalpa flowers tower, topple,/Cast a round white shadow in their dying . . .', 'A body of whiteness,/Rots, and smells of rot under its headstone/Though the body walk out in clean linen'. The opposition is a more complex one than that suggested by the primary contrasts of ripeness and sterility because fertility itself implicitly involves death: 'Death whitens in the egg and out of it.' White, with its developed qualities of sterility and death, also has emotional significance: 'It is a complexion of the mind.' The first ten verses dwell on the inter-related images; the last two verses explain the allusion of the title. Lucina, the moon goddess, is the source of all whiteness, her frankness is a cruelty which reduces man to her own bony, elemental starkness. The purple skin and red blood of the berries intrude into the white universe with sinister power:

> Lucina, bony mother, labouring
> Among the socketed white stars, your face
> Of candour pares white flesh to the white bone,
>
> Who drag our ancient father at the heel,
> White-bearded, weary. The berries purple
> And bleed. The white stomach may ripen yet.

In these two verses for the first time we find several of the later typical associations of the moon—'Bony mother' finds echoes in 'The moon is my mother' and 'The moon has nothing to be sad about,'Staring from her hood of bone'. The moon is associated with the stars in 'Insomniac' and is frequently visualised as a face: 'that mad hard face'; 'The moon is no door. It is a face in its own right'; 'Under the eyes of the stars and the moon's rictus'; 'The moon lays a hand on my forehead./Blank-faced and mum as a nurse'. The relationship between the barren white moon and red, with which Sylvia Plath often associates fertility, hinted at in the last verse of 'Moonrise', is developed at greater length in the later poems. In 'Moonrise' a detailed symbolic value is given to the moon as the source of whiteness and death, decay, aridity, cruelty and infertility. The poem, which has begun to internalise the perceived external details and relate them more immediately to experiences of the mind, is one of the first important poems in the transition period between early and mature work. It seems significant that this development is accompanied by a new complexity of imagery and allusion; in fact it could be said of 'Moonrise' that the greater depth of the poem results from the new solidity of reference.

The long 'Poem For a Birthday' has few typical images, largely because it borrows Roethke's distinctive plant and animal imagery, but the only reference to the moon is a valuable one:

> Lady, who are these in the moon's vat—
> Sleepdrunk, their limbs at odds?
> In this light the blood is black.
> Tell me my name.

The moon is here seen as a controlling female power which can affect identity, a conception which also figures in many of the later poems. The only suggestion that the moon's powers can be in any way limited occurs in 'The Rival': 'The moon too abases her subjects/But in the daytime she is ridiculous.' This daytime relief is incidental to the poetry though as the predominant world of Sylvia Plath's poetry is a nocturnal one where the white menace of the moon reigns powerfully. In a talk prepared for the BBC but never broadcast Sylvia Plath said of her later poetry:[2]

2. Alvarez, *op. cit.*, p. 59.

These new poems of mine have one thing in common.
They were all written at about four in the morning—
that still, blue, almost eternal hour before the baby's
cry, before the glassy music of the milkman, settling
his bottles.

Moon imagery plays an increasing part in the transitional
poems published in magazines and journals in 1960 and 1961 and
now collected, in part, in Crossing the Water. In 'Candles' the
moon is described as 'bald', a description which is also used in
the later 'The Moon and the Yew Tree'. It seems reasonable to
associate 'bald' with age, but this is not the major association
which the word carries in Sylvia Plath's poetry—rather it carries
the sense of bare, plain, unadorned, stark: 'The lines of your eye,
scalded by these bald surfaces'; 'this relic saved/Face, to face the
bald-faced sun'; 'A bald angel blocks and shapes/The flying
light'; 'The midwife slapped your footsoles, and your bald cry/
Took its place among the elements'. The consistency with which
the word is used in bleak, terrifying and oppressive situations
lends it sinister connotations. In this connection particularly noteworthy is its value in 'The Disquieting Muses', in which Sylvia
Plath describes the forces behind her poetry in terms of stone-
gowned women: 'Nodding by night around my bed,/Mouthless,
eyeless, with stitched bald head.' She achieves a terrifying synthesis
of blankness, unknown menace, ugliness and fear here and the
word 'bald' is central to the image. Similar conceptions can be
found in the very late poetry: 'A world of bald white days in a
hadeless socket'; 'Those mannequins lean tonight/In Munich,
morgue between Paris and Rome,/Naked and bald in their furs,
/Orange lollies on silver sticks,/Intolerable, without mind'. Bald-
ness is also connected with blindness; a blindness which is both
physical, in 'The Colossus'—'The bald, white tumuli of your
eyes'—and spiritual, in 'Love Letter':

You didn't just toe me an inch, no—
Nor leave me to set my small bald eye,
Skyward again, without hope, of course,
Of apprehending blueness, or stars.

A tenuous relationship is established in 'Candles' between the 'bald moon' and the candles which, with their softer light, 'mollify' the moon, but in 'Mirror' the moon and the candles are grouped together as liars in contrast to the truthfulness of the mirror:

> Now I am a lake. A woman bends over me,
> Searching my reaches for what she really is.
> Then she turns to those liars, the candles and the moon.

Mirrors occur frequently in Sylvia Plath's poetry but with a variety of meanings so that it is difficult to define any final value for the mirror as a symbol. An early poem, 'In Midas' Country',[3] uses the mirror as a visual image for the surface of a river:

> But now the water skiers race,
> Bracing their knees. On unseen towlines
> They cleave the river's greenish patinas;
> The mirror quivers to smithereens.

Even in this simple instance the mirror has further connotations; an earlier verse has stated with typical ambivalence: 'It might be heaven, this static plenitude . . .' The eruption of the skiers into the scene disrupts the static peace, thus the image of the broken mirror reflects the destruction of spiritual as well as physical calm. This destruction of peace is eventually accepted, even exulted in, in 'The Couriers': 'A disturbance in mirrors,/The sea shattering its grey one—/Love, love, my season.' 'Words', written in the last week of her life, has a further image of the calm surface of water as a mirror:

> The sap
> Wells like tears, like the
> Water striving
> To re-establish its mirror
> Over the rock
>
> That drops and turns,
> A white skull,
> Eaten by weedy greens.

3. 'In Midas' Country', *London Magazine*, 6, October 1959, p. 11.

This use of the word strongly indicates that one important value of the mirror as a symbol in Sylvia Plath's poetry lies in its representation of a state of normality and safety, and this is the sense which informs its use in 'Brasilia': '. . . leave/This one/Mirror safe, unredeemed/By the dove's annihilation,/The glory,/The power, the glory.'

The mirror can also be a symbol of the personality. It can suggest wisdom: '. . . and this is the surgeon:/One mirrory eye—/A facet of knowledge'; monotony: 'His head is a little interior of grey mirrors' and it is associated with the monotonous, inevitable, unchanging process of living in 'Totem':

> There is no terminus, only suitcases
>
> Out of which the same self unfolds like a suit
> Bald and shiny, with pockets of wishes,
>
> Notions and tickets, short circuits and folding mirrors.

In 'Morning Song' the mirror forms part of an image of pregnancy and in 'Childless Woman' becomes a reflection of the attempt to conceive. In 'A Birthday Present', a late, rather desperate death-wish poem, it is seen as a symbol of death:

> Do not be mean, I am ready for enormity.
> Let us sit down at it, one on either side, admiring the gleam,
>
> The glaze, the mirrory variety of it.

The only general conclusion which can be drawn from the very varied uses of the mirror as a symbol is that, as in 'A Birthday Present', it usually represents an absolute state from which or in which the poet strives to find a meaning. This is the value which it conveys in the late poem 'Mirror':

> I am silver and exact. I have no preconceptions.
> Whatever I see I swallow immediately
> Just as it is, unmisted by love or dislike.
> I am not cruel, only truthful—
> The eye of a little god, four-cornered.

The persona seeks to locate in the mirror a definition or

confirmation of her sense of being which she cannot find in the falsifying light of either the candles or the moon:

> Now I am a lake. A woman bends over me,
> Searching my reaches for what she really is.
> Then she turns to those liars, the candles or the moon.
> I see her back, and reflect it faithfully.

The last part of this verse indicates that the mirror is a symbol in Sylvia Plath's poetry not of the Platonic ideal but of the real itself: it is a measure of the exact, objective truth and it records the daily progress towards death. In fact the mirror can be a symbol for the individual life itself; and in 'Contusion', written in the last week of her life, it is for this reason that: 'The mirrors are sheeted.'

To return to the moon as a symbol in Sylvia Plath's poetry, we find that 'Insomniac' hints at the moon's hostility—'Under the eye of the stars and the moon's rictus'—and this is a theme which is developed with increasing fierceness in *Ariel*: 'The moon also is merciless'; 'The moon is my mother. She is not sweet like Mary'; 'The moon too abases her subjects'. Finally in 'Edge' the persona enters the world of the moon and her hostility is reduced to acceptance: 'The moon has nothing to be sad about,/Staring from her hood of bone./She is used to this sort of thing.' 'Surgeon at 2 a.m.' reinforces the suggestions of suffering associated with the moon by introducing it into the world of hospitals, illness and blood: 'The red night lights are flat moons./They are dull with blood.' An almost identical image occurs in 'Three Women': 'The night lights are flat red moons. They are dull with blood.' This insistence on the moon as 'flat' is echoed in 'Elm' where the flatness is the result of major surgery to remove a diseased part. The conception of the moon as diseased is a common one in the later poetry.

'Heavy Women' initiates what is to be the major symbolic value of the moon in the later poetry: 'Over each weighty stomach a face/Floats calm as a moon or a cloud.' This is in fact an untypical relationship between the moon and fertility; the moon's significance is usually as a force of infertility opposed to the human fertility of the woman who conceives and gives birth, as in 'Three Women', 'She is simply astonished at fertility.' The barren moon is more actively hostile in 'Elm': 'She would drag me cruelly being barren.' 'The Munich Mannequins' gives a symbolic value to the moon as an indication of the menstrual flow which is a monthly sign of sterility:

> Perfection is terrible, it cannot have children.
> Cold as snow breath, it tamps the womb

> Where the yew trees blow like hydras,
> The tree of life and the tree of life

> Unloosing their moons, month after month, to no purpose.
> The blood flood is the flood of love,

In this poem the moon and the yew tree are connected in an image of physical sterility which is reminiscent of 'The Moon and the Yew Tree', a poem about spiritual sterility and despair. A further instance of the yew tree as a symbol of blackness, despair and sterility can be found in 'Little Fugue', where it is also associated with the poet's father.

The moon is again associated with sterility in 'The Other':

> Navel-cords, blue-red and lucent,

> Shriek from my belly like arrows, and these I ride.
> O moon-glow, o sick one,

> The stolen horses, the fornications
> Circle a womb of marble.

Sterility is regarded as a disease and the moon is a symbol of both disease and infertility. In 'Thalidomide' the deformed child, conceived by the life-giving forces of love, has been affected by the diseased sterility of the moon:

> O half moon—

> Half-brain, luminosity—
> Negro, masked like a white,

> Your dark
> Amputations crawl and appal—

The moon is black but masked as white. Throughout Sylvia Plath's poetry the moon is consistently associated with an extreme whiteness which carries no connotations of virginity, purity, or innocence, but which is indicative of sterility, disease, alienation and despair. It is also occasionally associated with the colour blue, which often suggests an actively hostile quality, as in 'Three Women':

> How long can I be
> Gentling the sun with the shade of my hand,
> Intercepting the blue bolts of a cold moon?

Perhaps the most remarkable and allusive example of image clusters associated with the moon occurs in 'Three Women' as the Secretary, who has just experienced the most recent of several miscarriages, muses on the moon:

> I feel it enter me, cold, alien, like an instrument.
> And that mad, hard face at the end of it,
>   that O-mouth
> Open in its gape of perpetual grieving.
> It is she that drags the blood-black sea around
> Month after month, with its voices of failure.
> I am helpless as the sea at the end of her string.

The moon is here associated with hospitals and illness, with sterility, madness, grief, the sea, fertility, despair and blood. It is seen as a face with an O-mouth and is personified as a female. This passage exemplifies the many values of the moon as a symbol in Sylvia Plath's work. Generally we can conclude that the moon's world is a feminine one which is sterile, bald, wild, hostile but grieving; it is a world of physical and spiritual suffering opposed to the worlds of fertility, holiness, tenderness and love. It is a world towards which the poems inexorably move as the poet increasingly claims kinship with the forces of blackness and suffering: 'It drags the sea after it like a dark crime; it is quiet/With the O-gape of complete despair. I live here.'

Ultimately the moon represents death and, as has been noted, in 'Edge' Sylvia Plath moves towards a fusion of the worlds of love and tenderness symbolised by her children and that of the moon. The poems have ceased to resist the compulsive darkness of the moon by eventually entering that darkness. The long struggle is over.

Select Bibliography

I. Sylvia Plath

1. Published Works

Ariel. London (Faber and Faber) 1965; New York (Harper Bros.) 1966.
Crossing the Water. London (Faber and Faber) 1971.
The Bell Jar. By 'Victoria Lucas', London (Heinemann) 1963.
The Bell Jar. By Sylvia Plath, London (Faber and Faber) 1966.
The Colossus. London (Heinemann) 1960; New York (Alfred Knopf) 1962; London (Faber and Faber) 1967.
Three Women. (Turret Press) 1968. Limited edition of 150 copies.
Uncollected Poems. (Turret Press) 1965. Limited edition of 150 copies.
Winter Trees. London (Faber and Faber) 1971.

2. Prose in Periodicals

'Context', in *London Magazine*, 2 (n.s.), February 1962, pp. 45–6.
'Ocean 1212-W', in *The Listener*, 29 August 1963, pp. 312–13.

2. Biographical and Critical

Alvarez, A. 'Sylvia Plath', in *The Review*, 1: 9, October 1963, pp. 20–6.
——'Beyond All This Fiddle', in *Times Literary Supplement*, 23 March 1967, pp. 229–32.
——*The Savage God*, London (Weidenfeld and Nicolson) 1971.

Cox, C. B. and Jones, A. R. 'After the Tranquillized Fifties', *Critical Quarterly*, 6, 1964, pp. 107–22.

Hamilton, Ian. 'Sylvia Plath', in *London Magazine*, 3 (n.s.), 1963, pp. 54–6.

Holbrook, David. 'The 200 inch Distorting Mirror', *New Society*, 11 July 1968, pp. 57–8.

——'R. D. Laing and the Death Circuit', *Encounter*, 31, 2 August 1968, pp. 35–45.

Homberger, Eric. *A Chronological Checklist of the Periodical Publications of Sylvia Plath*, University of Exeter American Arts Documentation Centre, England, 1970.

Jones, A. R. 'Necessity and Freedom: The Poetry of Robert Lowell, Sylvia Plath and Anne Sexton', *Critical Quarterly*, 7, 1965, pp. 11–30.

Newman, Charles. (ed.) *The Art of Sylvia Plath: A Symposium*, London (Faber and Faber) 1970.

Orr, Peter. (ed.) *The Poet Speaks*, London (Routledge and Kegan Paul) 1966.

Rosenthal, M. L. *The New Poets: American and British Poetry Since World War 2*, New York (Oxford University Press) 1967.